THE ULTIMATE GUIDE TO

SUMMER
OPPORTUNITIES

FOR TEENS

THE ULTIMATE GUIDE TO

SUMMER OPPORTUNITIES

FOR TEENS

200 PROGRAMS THAT PREPARE YOU FOR COLLEGE SUCCESS

SANDRA L. BERGER

PRUFROCK PRESS INC.
WACO, TEXAS

Library of Congress Cataloging-in-Publication Data

Berger, Sandra L.
 The ultimate guide to summer opportunities for teens : 200 programs that prepare you for college suc-
cess / Sandra L. Berger.
    p. cm.
 Includes bibliographical references and index.
 ISBN-13: 978-1-59363-235-9 (pbk.)
 ISBN-10: 1-59363-235-5
 1. Vacation schools—United States—Directories. 2. Summer schools—United States—Directories. 3.
High school students—United States. 4. College student orientation—United States. I. Title.
 LC5715.B47 2008
 373.12'3202573—dc22
                              2007029647

Copyright © 2008 Prufrock Press Inc.
Edited by Lacy Elwood
Cover and Layout Design by Marjorie Parker

ISBN-13: 978-1-59363-235-9
ISBN-10: 1-59363-235-5

Printed in the United States of America.

At the time of this book's publication, all facts and figures cited are the most current available. All tele-
phone numbers, addresses, and Web site URLs are accurate and active. All publications, organizations,
Web sites, and other resources exist as described in the book, and all have been verified. The authors
and Prufrock Press Inc. make no warranty or guarantee concerning the information and materials given
out by organizations or content found at Web sites, and we are not responsible for any changes that
occur after this book's publication. If you find an error, please contact Prufrock Press Inc.

Prufrock Press Inc.
P.O. Box 8813
Waco, TX 76714-8813
Phone: (800) 998-2208
Fax: (800) 240-0333
http://www.prufrock.com

CONTENTS

ACKNOWLEDGEMENTS

The author appreciates the assistance of Lacy Elwood, my very capable editor, and Kate Sepanski, the intern at Prufrock Press who set up the database and took care of technical aspects. Without their energy and skill, this book would not exist.

PART I:

WHAT YOU NEED TO KNOW BEFORE CHOOSING A SUMMER PROGRAM

INTRODUCTION

There are more than 200 programs listed in *The Ultimate Guide to Summer Opportunities for Teens*.

Each program agreed to be listed and provided the descriptive information. I have not visited these programs, so you will want to do some research and/or visit the programs when they are in session. I wanted to give you enough useful information so that you can look for summer programs that might be interesting and educational, and then follow through on your own. There are thousands of summer programs in the United States, so if you can't find something you like, don't give up. The universities in your area are a good resource for additional programs.

This book is written for and to students and their families. It is addressed to students and provides both information and background on topics that should interest them. Parents will be interested in the same information, but may take the most interest in the sections on paying for and choosing a program. Bright students have specific intellectual and social/emotional needs over and above other students. The programs listed in this book take account of those needs.

The program section is listed in a state-by-state order, with programs listed alphabetically within each state. In addition, a cross-index in Appendix A provides a list of all programs according to program type. You have two options in using this book: You can search only for programs in your state or general region, or you may search for programs nationwide within a certain discipline or topic of study.

Each listing includes a program's contact information and a brief program description. Each program listing includes a Web site that you can use to find further information on that program. If the Web site does not answer your questions, you should write to the program based on the contact information provided, and not to Prufrock Press.

Note that some of the programs have very *early deadlines*. Some fill up for the next season as soon as the program ends. So, be aware of early deadlines, especially if you need financial assistance. I hope you find something fun to do that will help you grow and prepare for your future. Happy hunting!

CHAPTER 1

A NEW WAY TO LOOK AT SUMMER VACATION

Do you have a passion to work side-by-side with a microbiologist 8 hours a day? Collaborate with playwrights and directors to produce a new play? Be immersed in the world of music? Write for 12 hours a day, creating short stories, poems, essays, or a weekly newspaper? Study the ecosystems of coral reefs on daily dives in the Caribbean? Build a wooden sea kayak and paddle it along the Maine coast for 3 weeks? Go to space camp and learn from the astronauts? Learn to speak Arabic, Chinese, or Portuguese? These are all possible pursuits during the summer months.

You're probably asking yourself: Why would I go to a summer program when I could lounge poolside or hang out with my friends? Your parents are probably asking: Why would I send my child to an expensive summer program? Here's why.

THE NEED FOR FREEDOM TO LEARN THROUGH EXPERIENCE

Summer is downtime. Summer is a time for reflection and using your time in ways that are both fulfilling and fun. Somehow the schedule seems less rigid, although we may be just as busy as the school year. Choosing our own activities and doing something we love makes the days and weeks fly by, especially if that something is challenging. The days are longer, giving us more daylight hours. There is the feeling of less pressure. No one is looking over your shoulder, reminding you that time is passing.

There is no other time during the year for total immersion—to immerse oneself in a self-selected activity and focus solely on that topic, to travel and meet people from other cultures, to become more linguistically, culturally, and globally aware. There is no better time to explore your interests or acquire skills that will serve you for the rest of your life. You can accelerate through an academic course with people who are as interested as you are and can work at a rapid pace. Or, you can explore a new topic not taught in school, such as archeology or paleontology, that might ultimately lead to a college major or career. You can spend the summer learning about performing arts or computer animation. The structure and pace are yours to choose.

The learning that takes place during the summer is special. You can choose to take intellectual risks, to play with ideas, to write prose or poetry, to ask questions, to be in tune with nature. You can look at history in new ways or solve problems in new situations. There's a certain amount of risk attached to trying new things, digging into the unknown, and playing with ideas. It's risky to stretch yourself, reaching higher than you thought you could go. You might become a more interesting person. Summer is special. It's a gift of time during which you can transform yourself by building on your strengths and developing new ones. It's an opportunity to be part of an in-depth, concentrated learning experience of whatever you choose. And, if you plan ahead, you can spend the summer with people who are interested in the same activities and who have a passion for learning and sharing.

If you ask an adult about pleasant childhood memories, many will talk about one particular summer that made a life-changing difference where learning was fun—a once-in-a-lifetime experience. When I was 16, I spent 9 weeks camping with a group across the United States, going to climbing school in the Rocky Mountains, learning how to recover an upended canoe in the Ely River, horseback riding along a trail, watching a beautiful sunset in the Grand Teton Park, and sailing a schooner from Bellingham, WA, to Victoria, Canada. I learned about the country, about my fellow teenage travelers, and most importantly, I learned about myself. In addition, I acquired the skills to survive in the outdoors by myself and felt more independent than when I left home.

Summer programs help us learn about communal living, acquire skills that will serve us for many years, participate in challenging courses that are paced for rapid learners, accelerate through courses that might otherwise be boring, focus in one area for weeks at a time, and take the time to think about what new areas might interest us. During the summer, in an appropriate course or program, there are opportunities for intellectual problem solving. There are countless opportunities for an exciting experience.

THE NEED FOR ADVANCED INSTRUCTION

Students who study music or the arts require early and advanced lessons in order to develop their full potential. The same is true of students who have talents in academic subjects like science and mathematics. These students need mentors who can answer their questions and an intellectual peer group who can stimulate their thinking. The peer group has its own energy and is sometimes just as important as the teaching. The need for advanced learning simply cannot be fulfilled during the school year. Even the most energetic teacher can't spend enough time with students who have a thirst for learning.

THE NEED FOR DOWNTIME AND BALANCE

During the academic semester, most teens lead a very hectic life, trying to fit extracurricular activities in a calendar that is already loaded with high-powered courses. Their calendars present an intimidating display of appointment dates and times. They are offended when adults tell them they are doing too much. Summer is a great time to try out new activities that you don't have time for during the school year. Just getting away from the normal day-to-day structure provides opportunities to explore and imagine. New activities and a change of pace can help you develop untried skills and expand your ideas about who you are and what you can accomplish. This is particularly important for college-bound teens because when you look at college applications, you will find that one of the things colleges want to know is, "What are your strengths and what have you accomplished?" The question may be difficult to answer because we don't often think about our strengths or weak areas. Summer enrichment programs present an opportunity for self-discovery where you can test yourself and have fun with new challenges in an environment where no one is judging you and pressure is minimized. You can afford to put less pressure on yourself and be less perfectionistic than you are during the school year. The goal during the summer should be to enjoy what you are doing—to enjoy life.

THE NEED FOR ADVENTURE
AND EXPLORATION

Middle school students in particular crave adventure. If you are a middle school student, you may be interested in the protection of natural resources and the recycling of waste. You may be concerned about the decrease in population of white polar bears or whales. This does not mean that you feel self-confident in the outdoors. Many preteens and teens are intensely interested in global warming but may actually be uncomfortable around non-poisonous snakes, bugs, spiders, raccoons, plants you don't recognize, etc. Students in middle school and early high school are the perfect age for a program like Outward Bound. Adventure activities include rock climbing, kayaking, mountain biking, rappelling, caving, climbing wall, SCUBA diving, whitewater rafting, and many more outdoor adventure activities. Some students are reluctant to participate in these activities, so one of the goals is to learn from experts how to be safe when you are in the wild. When you were younger, you may have enjoyed academic activities and games and spent free time indoors. You preferred Sudoku to soccer, and reading to rafting or rock climbing. You identify yourself as someone who loves to think and solve problems. The importance of spending free time doing what you love cannot be overemphasized, but at some point it's important to spend time doing activities that are unfamiliar and challenging. So, if you are one of those teens who thinks that a hike in the woods is not cool, you may want to find outdoor activities that offer environmental awareness and get to know what Nature offers. In doing so, you might develop strengths that you were not aware of. It's time to stretch into a stronger you!

THE NEED FOR ENRICHMENT AND ACCELERATION

During the next few years, you may want to accelerate in one subject—usually math or a foreign language—or learn something entirely new like psychology, creative writing, archeology, or genealogy. You may want to take these courses with friends who read and comprehend quickly, especially if you spend a lot of time in classes waiting for others to catch up. A typical school day divided into 55-minute segments does not leave time for pursuing courses that are not typically taught in school, exploring a topic in depth, or playing with ideas. Teachers are responsible for testing, as well as subject matter, and many are not even given time for planning. Lots of bright students do not know how to take tests, but teaching kids to take tests is just not an option. Teachers must follow a state-approved syllabus, which can be very confining. Your teachers may not have time to make courses interesting or exciting. When some of your school classes lack energy or are just plain boring, finding an appropriate summer enrichment or acceleration opportunity might be one way to relight your intellectual fire. Another might be to take courses online from an accredited school or university.

There are literally hundreds of places to look for enrichment. Your own school system is an excellent resource for finding appropriate summer programs. The cost of school-sponsored enrichment may be more reasonable than the cost of private programs. You can find these courses by calling your school system's Office of Instruction and asking about summer courses. Some school systems ask the city's Department of Parks and Recreation or Adult Education to sponsor credit courses. Do you live near a university? Most states have at least one university that offers enrichment to students during the summer. The four regional talent search programs offer academic acceleration and enrichment at the Center for Talented Youth (CTY) at Johns Hopkins University in Maryland, the Talent Identification Program (TIP) at Duke University in North Carolina, Rocky Mountain Talent Search (RMTS) at the University of Denver in Colorado, and the Center for Talent Development (CTD) at Northwestern University in Illinois. Between these four talent searches, students throughout the entire United States have access to talent identification services, publications, and educational programs, including enrichment. Additional programs are listed in this book. Honors and Advanced Placement courses are typically accelerated; that is, presented in half the number of hours as scheduled by a normal school semester.

THE NEED FOR INDEPENDENCE

Young people need a variety of experiences, especially during the teen years. Most teens also want and need to lessen their dependence on their parents, form separate identities, and stand on their own feet. Summer is the ideal time for learning responsible ways of becoming independent; camp or some other summer activity provides a wholesome escape from home, school, friends, and expectations. Kids have the freedom to be themselves in an environment that is more flexible and offers a change of pace, environment, and context. There are many different types of summer activities where you will have a good time and learn something new or improve a favorite activity. This book, for students and parents, is a guide to programs that emphasize learning opportunities of all types. These opportunities have one thing in common—they are designed for preteens or teens and there is something for everyone.

GROWTH IN SELF-ESTEEM

Based on research, we know that students who were accelerated in mathematics at an early age experienced an increase in self-esteem that was directly related to the acceleration. This effect of acceleration has been seen across many academic disciplines (Davidson & Davidson, 2004). Attending an appropriate summer program that provides acceleration is one way for college-bound students to gain academic self-confidence. Moving through a course at your own pace is empowering socially, as well as emotionally. Rapidly paced summer programs can give you a feeling of accomplishment and increased control over your life. We also know that when teens research summer programs, decide with their families how and where they want to spend the summer months, take responsibility for planning and preparing, and, finally, earn some or all of the money to pay for it, the end result is growth-promoting. If you succeed in doing something you were not sure you could do, you are likely to see yourself in a new light. Your parents will appreciate your growing independence and sense of responsibility.

It may be important to tell your parents that children who attended a summer program where they found friends like themselves and interesting activities say that they benefited in many ways, including (American Camp Association, 2005):

- growth in confidence and increased self-esteem,
- ability to make new friends,
- growth of independence and leadership skills, and
- willingness to try new things and participate in adventurous activities.

LEARNING THROUGH SUMMER EXPERIENCES

COMMUNAL LIVING

If you are planning to spend your summer in a residential program, you will be part of a large community, perhaps on a university campus. Communal living is quite unlike living with your family. In communal living, you are more independent than you are at home, most of the choices you make have a direct impact on your peer group, and you are responsible for those choices. At home, if you are not tidy, your parents may remind you to pick up your things. Living away from home, your group is not likely to be so courteous. There are negative consequences if you don't treat members of your group well. Cooperation is one of the first things teens learn when living with other teens. Kids meet new challenges and conquer fears with peer group support and a sense that they belong to a community.

CAREER TESTING AND BUILDING

If you are thinking about careers, like most college bound students, this is the perfect time to do some testing and experimenting. Summer is a great time to start building credentials that will later open the door to new opportunities. When you apply to colleges, you will be asked about your interests and passions. If you can show that your interests began when you were young and have developed over time (establishing a track record), if you have participated in competitions or shown some leadership in your interest areas, you will lay the groundwork for building credentials. (We'll say more about credentials in the next chapter of this book.)

For example, a student whom we'll call Isabel wanted to go into broadcasting. She thought she had some of the necessary people skills and loved the idea of appearing in front of a camera. Isabel and her mother went to a local television station so Isabel could look for volunteer opportunities. She persuaded a producer to give her an opportunity as an intern, and worked there all summer. She learned about life behind the scenes and discovered that broadcasting was a lot less glamorous than she imagined. This experience served her well, and she took advantage of other opportunities to volunteer in similar places. When Isabel applied to college, because of her experiences, she had decided her major and knew that she wanted to enter the field of advertising. She had the background to persuade the college to accept her application and offer some financial aid.

Another student, Karl, was really good at mathematics and he knew that he wanted to take calculus and statistics in high school. He also knew that 4 years of high school did not give him time to do everything that interested him. So, Karl took algebra during the summer after seventh grade, and made sure that he had the documentation that his high school required to give him credit. He took geometry during the summer after eighth grade. By the time he reached 11th grade, he was able to take advanced math courses at the local college.

There are many students like Karl who, for a variety of reasons, want to accelerate through middle and high school, particularly in subjects they are good at. By using the summer months during middle school, they set the stage for doing just that. Just as you would try several pairs of shoes to see which is the best fit, trying on a career for size will make you most comfortable later on. For advanced students, summer can be a rich gold mine of opportunities, whether you are taking academic courses, acquiring leadership skills, traveling, helping those less fortunate by volunteering, working in a laboratory like the one at the Naval Observatory, participating in research, honing athletic skills, or getting involved in the arts. The right summer program can become part of the architecture of your life.

Getting Credit

Some students accelerate by taking out-of-school courses they would normally take during the school year. There are many summer academic courses that will grant either high school or college credit. However, many high schools will not accept credit earned in a summer program *not sponsored* by your school district. Some high schools will not place an accelerated student in the next course in the sequence. For example, if you take algebra or geometry and excel, it's reasonable to expect that in the fall, you will be able to sign up for the next math course in the sequence. What is reasonable to expect may be counter to your school district's policy. Many schools are concerned about their offerings when a student has accelerated and finishes an academic sequence as a sophomore or junior. The instructional staff may fear being pressured to offer advanced courses for only a few students by a limited teaching staff. Thus, schools may discourage students from taking out-of-school courses because of the long-term consequences. Because this is not uncommon, you must discuss the consequences with your school before your family spends a lot of money on a summer course. If you and your parents want to try convincing your school district that acceleration works, a publication and Web site that provides significant research can be found at http://www.nationdeceived.org.

Perhaps you can get the courses you need online, through either a university or one of the talent search programs mentioned earlier. Although I would not recommend this path, it may be helpful to know that many universities will enroll young students with no high school diploma if the student can prove that he or she is capable of college-level work. You can accomplish this by taking a few online courses at a local college. The other thing you should know is that colleges are less enthusiastic than they used to be about AP courses, and some will give credit or placement only to those who have scored a 5 on an AP test.

CHAPTER 2

COLLEGE PLANNING: TAKE A DRY RUN THIS SUMMER

Enrolling in a residential academic summer program that takes place on a college campus will give you a taste of college life. Think of it as a dry run that will expose you to pathways that are helpful and hazards to avoid. You will get the feel of a college campus as a community. You will live in a dormitory with other students, eat with them in the dining hall, and use the campus library. On your way to the dining hall or library, read the notices on the wall. Are students passionate about politics? Do they care about the same things that you care about? Read the college newspaper. Most campuses have wireless networks and connecting your personal computer is simple. But, also check to see if there are computer labs, especially if you are interested in computer programming. If you think you might be a science major, visit the science labs when students are there. Check to see how many students use each microscope or other equipment and ask who teaches the lab courses. Of course, there is more to school than classes, so be sure to check out the weekend scene. Where is the nearest theater with first-run movies or popular music concerts? At some schools, students must find transportation to the nearest town to see a movie. But, in some cases, they are not allowed to have cars until sophomore or junior year and there is no public transportation. If that makes a big difference to you and you would not want to be in that position, you have learned something about yourself, as well as something to look for at other colleges. When you select colleges to apply to, you will have an advantage if you have lived on different types of campuses during the summer. You will know what and who to look for and how to orient yourself.

Eventually you will need to figure out the differences and similarities among different types of colleges and universities (e.g., small private liberal arts, technical schools, teaching/research universities, large state universities), and decide where you feel most comfortable. How is Cal Tech different from MIT, the University of Michigan, or North Carolina State University? If you want a career in technology or engineering, it's a good idea to figure out how the programs at those four schools differ from one another. College courses are different than high school courses in many ways. First, in college you have more choices. You can choose not to go to class and deal with the consequences. Second, someone—either you or your parents—has paid for the courses. Teachers are different. In high school, your teachers know who you are and will applaud your efforts. On a large campus with large classes, faculty members may not have a clue about you. If you get to know them, it will be because you made an effort. If you like anonymity, that can be an advantage. But, if you need to like a teacher in order to make good grades, check out a smaller campus environment. Some colleges have tutorial classes and seminars for freshmen students. Some colleges offer a trimester system where you can study fewer courses for a shorter period of time. The end result in credits earned is the same as the more typical system where you take five courses each semester, but students have more time to focus on each course or topic. While you are on campus for a summer residential program, talk to students and ask what they liked and disliked about their courses and experiences. At a later time, you might talk to professionals in the field that interests you to ask which college courses were most useful and which were a total waste of time.

SELECTIVITY

Selectivity is an issue for all college applicants. It has to do with the ratio of the number of applicants to a specific college versus the number of students accepted and by extension, the rigor of the courses. A university that accepts one student out of every 10 or 15 applicants is highly selective. Harvard, Princeton, Yale, MIT, and most of the Ivy League schools (called "Ivies") are all highly selective. Selectivity is one of the most important factors in choosing a college because it tells you what your acceptance chances are and, if enrolled, how hard you will have to work. A highly selective school is likely to attract highly competitive students. Until a few years ago, the ratio of applicants to acceptances (e.g., 10 applicants to 1 accepted) was the best way to assess the level of challenge. Now however, there is a different method to assess schools, developed by the National Survey of Student Engagement (NSSE). Their Web site is http://nsse.iub.edu/pdf/survey_instruments/NSSE_2003_survey.pdf.

The NSSE asked students 30 questions about their classes such as, "How often did you prepare two or more drafts of a paper?" The answers fall in a range from *very often* to *never*. Looking at the survey, you will quickly see that students who take rigorous challenging classes are going to answer one way and students who take easy classes will answer an entirely different way. The survey was not developed for this use, so you may be wondering how this helps you look at colleges. First, the survey responses for each school gives you the level of challenge. Second, the survey responders were students who had to gauge the rigor of their courses. This method of gauging the rigor of courses is a lot more accurate than information provided in the many college handbooks on the market. There are other college guides that provide student responses to questions about their school, but they do not look at the courses and level of challenge. For example, to compile *The Best 361 Colleges*, The Princeton Review asked more than 110,000 college students what their schools were really like. The "Best Party School" ranking list gets a lot of attention, but it is just one small part of this guide. Their survey is available at the following Web site: http://www.princetonreview.com/college/research/rankings/rankings.asp.

If you are thinking about applying to a selective college or university, the way you spend your summers is extremely important. Colleges want to know that you have chosen your summer activities wisely, developed your talents, and achieved success in highly rigorous courses. Experience is empowering. The more experiences you have, the better you will know what you can easily do and which activities are challenging. This may sound simplistic but it's not. Learning about yourself—your limits, as well as your successes—is ongoing and very complex but it can be fun.

If you aspire to a highly selective college, the following factors might give you an edge over equally competitive students. You may think you don't need an edge but there are more than 27,000 valedictorians each year. What if all or most of them wanted to attend the same college that interests you? Would your resume boost you to the top of the application pile?

- *Track Record (long time interest leading to true expertise):* This is where summer programs count the most. College admissions faculty are not going to be impressed if you do 10 or 12 things during high school. They are looking for activities that continued over several years. One university states: "We do not value one kind of extracurricular activity over another; in the long run, a student's depth of commitment to whatever they have chosen to pursue is more important to us than the length of their activity list" ("What Does Yale Look For?" 2007, ¶ 3). So, if you are interested in marine science, global warming, or oceanology, it is very important to spend your summers learning all you can from a variety of resources. Field research is particularly important. Woods Hole Oceanographic Institution in MA, one of the programs included in this book, states prominently on its Web site, "Preparation for a career in oceanography should begin as early as possible with a concentration in one scientific discipline. In high school, you should plan your studies around college-preparatory courses including math, English, science, and foreign languages. In college, you should choose a basic field of science in which to earn your first academic degree" ("How Can I Get a Job in Oceanography?" 2004, ¶ 1).

- *Suitable Program Matching Student Goals*: Colleges want to see a match between your interests and goals and their offerings. For example, if your ultimate goal is International Business and you can show the different ways that you have become interested in the field—internships, volunteering, etc.—and if the college of your choice has an outstanding economics department, you have probably found a way to make yourself stand out as an applicant. However, keep in mind that there is a difference between padding your resume and engaging in activities because you have passion. Admission officers are trained to spot extracurricular activities that look good on your college application but don't really add anything substantive.

- *Compelling Need* (*a unique need only you can fill*): Colleges want to know how applicants will make a unique contribution to the school. For example, if you are a published poet and the school is known for its creative writing courses, you might be considered a "compelling" applicant. No one can tell you how to become a compelling applicant. That story can be written only by you.

- *Clear Goals*: If it is clear that your summers are part of a master plan, your career goals can give you an edge, particularly if those goals are demonstrated by a track record.

- *Prestige*: Ivies pride themselves on names and contributors. This is out of your control unless you have a huge trust fund. Do *not* get a letter of recommendation from an important person who doesn't know you well. *Do* get a letter of recommendation from one of the mentors you cultivated during summer activities, especially if that person knows your work well and can speak to your potential success.

- *Special Qualities:* Awards or competitions (e.g., Intel Science Talent Search), atypical career goals (e.g., male nurses), talent areas (e.g., playing the bagpipes, bassoon, or oboe). One selective college offers a scholarship to academically qualified students who can successfully audition for their competitive "pipe band" or who want to compete with their team of Highland dancers or drummers. Summer experiences help with these special qualities because they give an eligible candidate a boost. For example, if math is your passion, your participation in the Ross summer mathematics program (http://www.math.ohio-state.edu/ross) will make you stand out when you apply to colleges. If you are interested in intellectual challenge and have a passion for learning, the Telluride Association's sophomore (TASS) and junior (TASP) programs offer a summer educational experience with "challenges and rewards rarely encountered in secondary school or even college" ("What Is TASP?" n.d., ¶ 1).

- *A Contribution to the School*: Yale University displays prominently on its Web site the following: "In selecting a freshman class of 1300 from over 20,000 applicants each year, the Yale Admissions Committee attempts to answer two questions: "Who is likely to make the most of Yale's resources?" and "Who will contribute most significantly to the Yale community?" ("What Does Yale Look For?" 2007, ¶ 1). When you think about summer activities, it is important to enjoy yourself and to connect the experience to your personal growth by asking, "Why do I want to attend this program?"

BOLSTER TEST-TAKING SKILLS

How are your test-taking skills? If you are in middle school (seventh or eighth grade), it's a good idea to take the SAT or ACT. Your scores on either test may give you acceptance to one of the four regional talent search programs and the fast-paced courses they offer. In addition, most precollege academic summer programs want to see your SAT/ACT scores when you submit an application. Typically, eligible students have scored at levels comparable to college-bound seniors.

If your test-taking skills could use some help and you don't have time for a summer course, check out Prepme.com, an online SAT-preparation service (http://www.prepme.com) launched by students at Oxford University, Stanford University, and the University of Chicago. According to their Web site, they offer an adaptive course that adjusts to your strengths and weaknesses, making sure you focus on the areas where you can attain the greatest improvement, and provide personal tutors from Stanford or University of Chicago. (These are students that achieved top scores, and work with you personally to achieve great results.) PrepMe.com recently launched the first SAT preparation program created specifically for sixth, seventh, and eighth graders. PrepMe's Precocious Program (http://www.prepme.com/our-services/precocious-details.php) pairs middle school students with highly qualified tutors in preparation for the SAT. This is the first SAT preparation program designed to prepare students as early as sixth grade. They claim to help students gain acceptance to one of the four regional talent search programs.

If you are planning to take the PSAT/NMSQT (Preliminary Scholastic Assessment Test/National Merit Scholarship Qualifying Test) in 10th grade, you should spend some time becoming familiar with the test. The NMSQT is the qualifying test for becoming a National Merit Finalist and winning a scholarship if your 11th grade scores are high enough. The PSAT/NMSQT is practice for the real SAT, which many students will need to take in order to apply for college. The scores don't count until eleventh grade and you can learn a lot in a year, especially if you know the areas where you are weak. Some very bright students are terrible test takers, especially standardized timed tests like the ACTs and SATs. Although poor test-taking skills isn't the end of the world, it's important to score high enough on these tests that you don't become ineligible for programs and colleges that use standardized test scores as a criterion for admission. Schools that receive many thousands of applications sometimes make the first cut based on test scores. They use the average of your grade point average, class rank, and standardized test scores. You will want to make sure your scores are high enough so that you aren't eliminated immediately. If you are a poor test taker because you have a learning disability, there's a book you should look at: *Rock the SAT* by Michael Moshan, David Mendelsohn, and Michael Shapiro, and published by McGraw-Hill in 2006. The authors have structured the book around 13 songs they wrote for learning vocabulary. They believe that vocabulary is where students get hung up and that it's much easier to learn vocabulary to music (as opposed to flash cards). The vocabulary words chosen for the book are, according to the authors, the most commonly used words in the SAT. Another good study skills book for students with learning disabilities is *Becoming a Master Student* by Dave Ellis (2002).

SATS AND ACTS: TO PREP OR NOT TO PREP

If taking a prep course will boost your scores, do it! The average increase, according to instructors, is at least 100 points. You can increase your scores that much by knowing test-taking tricks. It's reasonable to take the SAT or ACT three times, once during middle school and twice during high school. However, three times should be your limit. Beyond that, it's really a waste of your time because you are not likely to increase your score enough to make a big difference to the colleges. The exception is using a test prep program. If you have taken the test twice in high school and your scores do not reflect your ability and knowledge, by all means take a good prep course. Students who live in the Midwest generally take the ACT test, which colleges use in a similar manner. There are several Web sites where you can take practice tests and one site where you can take a free preparation course (https://www.march2success.com/index.htm). If you have severe test anxiety, you should definitely take some kind of prep course at a time when you can focus and give it some attention—summer. Choose a course where the instructor will analyze your test results and tell you specifically how you can raise your scores.

COLLEGE APPLICATION PREP CAMPS

Did you know that there are a growing number of traditional and academic summer camps that will prepare students for the college application process? Most of these camps are located on college campuses so you can glimpse a peek of campus life while you are there. Campers spend their time working on SAT or ACT preparation, academic workshops where you can bolster your strengths and work on your weaknesses, essay writing, mock admissions interviews, and other parts of the process. Some camps will give advice on specific colleges, depending on where the staff attended college. Campers are usually rising seniors who want to get a jump on the process. These camps are expensive and many people believe there are better ways to spend your summer, but if you decide such a camp is right for you, you may find such programs at http://www.mysummercamps.com or by conducting an online search for "college admission prep camp."

SUMMER ACTIVITIES SAY SOMETHING ABOUT YOU

When you complete college applications, the college will want to know who you are. Your grades and standardized test scores say one thing about you. Your extracurricular activities fill in the picture somewhat. But, colleges want to know what you are passionate about. They want to see a documentation of activities where you have honed your skills and some evidence that you can persevere. Colleges want to see commitment. They want to see leadership. When admissions officers sit down to look at an overwhelming pile of applications, they may give each applicant 5 or 10 minutes during the first run through. At that point, they divide applications into three piles—yes, no, and maybe. At the very least, you want to wind up in the maybe pile. You will need some credentials to demonstrate that you can successfully work at the college level. And, if you apply to a highly selective school, you may compete against 10,000 applicants. Even if your grades and standardized test scores put you at the top of the heap, you will need something else that answers the question, "Why should I admit you to this college?"

Some people believe that telling schools how you have overcome hardship is one of the keys to getting into a selective school. It's a myth. Schools want to see the results of your efforts. If you were a Dean of Admission, you would want to see that a student loves learning, enjoys new challenges, and knows how to set goals and succeed. Resiliency and overcoming hardship certainly counts, but only if you have a host of other qualities and can make it apparent as to how you will contribute to a college community. Students who are exposed to lots of different situations and activities are more interesting than students who spend all their time "making grades." Students who set realistic goals and gradually improve are seen as independent thinkers. Documentation counts. If you are a basement scientist, eventually you will have to test your mettle by demonstrating a project to people qualified to assess your work. If you are interested in writing, enter some contests every year and demonstrate how you have grown over time. If you can't afford a summer program, look for an online program. If you are interested in wind surfing, that is terrific, but admissions faculty will hardly be impressed unless you link wind surfing to an intense curiosity about physics, mathematics, or some other academic area and demonstrate that you are successful in those areas.

The earlier you can start planning for appropriate summer activities, the more time you will have until the end of high school. If you wait until high school, you have only three summers to learn what you can and accomplish your goals. The key is to plan ahead and understand the options.

CHAPTER 3

WHAT WILL YOU DO THIS SUMMER?

THE FAST-TRACK GENERATION

If you are younger than 16, you may not be able to remember what life was like before the Internet. You may not remember long-playing or 45 rpm records. As children of the Baby Boomers, today's teens are overprogrammed, overscheduled, and exhausted. Academic demands ratchet up as students take on more Advanced Placement courses or International Baccalaureate programs. In addition, a fast-growing, elite program is making its way to U.S. schools. The British-based University of Cambridge international program, which started to take root in the United States in the 1990s, is available in about 60 U.S. schools. The fall-out of taking excessive rigorous courses has, for some, come in the form of self-destructive behaviors such as eating disorders. A word of caution before we talk about programs: If you are overprogrammed and wondering if it is all worth it, staying home may not solve your problem. You may want to learn something that is purely fun, like photography, and avoid anything academically challenging during the summer. Your health is more important than your resume.

TYPES OF PROGRAMS

What are the connections between summer programs and college? As you look at the types of program opportunities, keep in mind that you are writing the story of *you*. The decisions you make have consequences beyond this summer, and hopefully will blend with your other choices to tell a story. So, if you tell colleges you want to major in foreign languages, taking AP language courses in high school during the regular semester makes sense. Building the story of you, during the weekends you might spend 3 hours every Saturday morning tutoring children who speak only Spanish. During the summer, if you can afford it, a trip to someplace in South America for a community service project will add additional substance to your experiences. If you can't afford travel or any other type of formal summer program, look around the city where you live for opportunities to help newly arrived immigrants to get basic services like food or education. The best way to do this is through your city's adult education or social service department. Perhaps you will be qualified to teach English or help in some other way. Summer is also a good time to find out if you *really* want to major in foreign languages. Too many adults find out too late that they are unhappy with their career choice. Consider summer a dress rehearsal and try a career on for size. Most importantly, I can't say strongly enough that you should never choose a program only because you think it will look good on your resume or impress the admissions committee. They need to know who you are, not who you pretend to be.

This section discusses the many different types of programs and provides information on several options, including both academic and adventurous opportunities. Keep in mind that two programs of the same type may be very different. Read the "fine print" so you will know what you are getting into. I have chosen not to include athletic programs in this book. If you are an athlete, your high school coach and teammates are a great source for information about summer activities in your sport.

We'll look at the following types of programs in the sections that follow:

- travel,
- gap year,
- academic enrichment or acceleration,
- fine and performing arts,
- service learning and youth leadership programs,
- volunteer programs, and
- internships.

TRAVEL

Summer travel programs offer you the opportunity to see some of the world, meet people from different countries, learn a new language, and live in a different culture. Travel gives you the opportunity to "try on a different you," to create that once-in-a-lifetime experience that might change your life. During college, you may have to spend summers earning money for the following academic year.

So, it's possible you may not have another opportunity to travel until you have finished college. Students who participate in travel programs often say they learn as much about their own views as they do about the topics they study, the people they meet, and the places they visit.

There are two types of travel programs: short-term and year-round. Short-term programs usually last several weeks during summer or school breaks; most require an adult chaperone. Some groups are sponsored by school systems or local universities. Lodging varies, depending on the program. Some school districts sponsor short-term overseas travel that is preceded by several weeks of summer school during which teens learn about the history and language of a country. Following travel, students are debriefed and have the opportunity to exchange photos and experiences. Year-round homestay programs are meant for students who wish to stay with a family in the country that interests them, attend language classes, and attend a local school. Some programs provide opportunities for high school and college students to participate in service projects in other countries.

HOMESTAY PROGRAMS

Many private companies specialize in sponsoring youth in different countries where they live with a host family. If travel takes place during the school semester, students have the opportunity to lead the typical day-to-day life of a high school age student in another country. It takes an open mind, a sense of humor, and flexibility to be a successful exchange student. (Keep in mind that you are not a tourist. You should not expect your homestay family to take you on a tour of the country.) However, the experiences leave students with greater confidence, maturity, and self-awareness, not to mention fluency in another language if you are there long enough and have the desire to learn.

There is much to think about if you want a homestay program, much more than this book can provide. The insurance issues are formidable, particularly because families need to find travel insurance that will offer protection if students need health or hospital care while they are abroad. For that reason, as well as others, finding a good consultant to help you select a program may save you time and confusion. One of the most important factors is the selection of a homestay family and their commitment to a visiting student. You need to make sure that if the homestay family has a change of heart because of changes in their family situation, the program will provide a carefully selected alternative family. Some organizations visit recommended host families in their homes while others use only recommendations and phone conversations. Some programs require host families to participate in an orientation, while others rely on printed material and conversations. You also will need at least one local program contact who will introduce you to your family and who knows how to proceed if there is a mismatch between you and the family. Make sure there is a solid support group in the country of your choice—people who are fluent in English, as well as the native language. As you can see, homestays are complex, which is why you would benefit from working with an independent consultant.

SUMMER TRAVEL

Choosing a summer travel program is challenging. You have to decide what type of program you want, the length of your stay, where you want to live, whether you want or need high school credit, and the size of the program. Think about your goals for a travel program. Here are some questions to consider as you do your research.

- *Leadership*: Is the leader experienced? The leadership for a short-term program is particularly critical to this type of trip. Each leader must be knowledgeable about the country and language and have experience working with teenagers. Check the qualifications each program requires of its leaders.

- *Activities*: The activities vary from program to program so read the itinerary carefully. Is enough time spent in each location to absorb some of its characteristics? Is there an extra cost for some activities?

- *Language*: The amount of time spent on language varies from program to program. Most short-term programs emphasize informal conversation and do not attempt a structured program. If perfecting a foreign language is your goal, look for a program that specializes in language study.

Some students start their search for summer travel with a particular country, but if you are not sure of what country to visit, you should check out the Web site of The Council on Standards for International Educational Travel (CSIET; http://www.csiet.org/mc/page.do). CSIET is a private, nonprofit organization whose mission is to identify reputable international youth exchange programs so that teens are provided with meaningful and safe international exchange experiences. They set standards for foreign study programs. They evaluate exchange programs to make certain that they adhere to certain practical and safety standards, and list all approved exchange organizations in the annual CSIET directory, the *Advisory List of International Educational Travel and Exchange Programs.* This directory is published as a service to schools, students, and host families. The *Advisory List* provides a resource from which prospective exchange students, their parents, and school leaders can confidently glean an understanding of the scope, background, and operations of programs that have been reviewed.

If programs on the CSIET list are not suitable, choose a well-known program that will let you talk to the students who have used that service. Most organizations have at least a few parents and alumni students who are willing to talk to prospective travelers. If they won't release any names, you should move on to a different organization. Programs like The Experiment in International Living (http://www.usexperiment.org) have been around for a long time and their Web site invites interested people to contact alumni. Resources for student travel can be found in Table 1.

GAP YEAR PROGRAMS

Most students head to college right after high school because that's the established path. Their parents expect it, they've taken the required classes, and all their friends are going. However, an increasing number of teens contemplating 4 more years of similar academic experiences in college elect to take a "gap year," a semester or academic year off from school to travel abroad, explore a career path by working or serving an internship, or commit to a program where they can help others who are less fortunate (e.g., Habitat for Humanity). And, some teens take a postgraduate year in school to prepare themselves academically for college classes.

Taking a gap year is a common practice in Europe, particularly England. This trend is growing in the United States, with many students taking time off before, during, or after college. Some highly selective colleges recommend it, understanding that bright intense students have been in an academic pressure cooker for years and need time out before jumping into a different but equally intense college experience. These colleges have found that students who take a gap year with specific goals "have it together." They return to school with renewed energy and motivation.

Students have many other reasons for taking a gap year. Those who did not get into their first choice college may want to make themselves more competitive by serving an internship or documenting their skills in a work environment. Some need to earn additional money for college, although most admissions counselors discourage students from delaying college to earn money. Anything a student earns will be counted when determining financial aid and may reduce the student's financial aid package. Some feel the urge to see some of the world before settling down to campus life. Some want the answer to the questions, "Why should I go to college?" and "What does college have to do with what I want in my life?" And, some want to contribute to a cause bigger than themselves. Whatever your reason for taking a gap year or semester, you will have to explain why you made the specific program choice and, like everything else, your reasons

TABLE 1: STUDENT TRAVEL RESOURCES

Council on Standards for International Educational Travel (CSIET)
http://www.csiet.org/mc/page.do

Glimpse Abroad
http://www.glimpseabroad.org/about.php

The Experiment in International Living
http:// www.usexperiment.org

Abbey Road Overseas Programs
http://www.goabbeyroad.com

The ASPECT Foundation Homestay Abroad Program
http://www.aspectfoundation.org/study_abroad/index.html

America's Adventure Ventures Everywhere
http://www.aave.com

Deer Hill Expeditions
http://www.deerhillexpeditions.com

Where There Be Dragons
http://www.wheretherebedragons.com

World Horizons International, LLC
http://www.world-horizons.com

ActionQuest
http://www.actionquest.com

Center for Cultural Interchange
http://www.cci-exchange.com

Global Crossroad
http://www.globalcrossroad.com

Living Routes Study Abroad in Ecovillages
http://www.LivingRoutes.org

Council on International Educational Exchange (CIEE)
http://www.ciee.org

Student Hosteling Program (SHP)
http://www.bicycletrips.com

The Cultural Immersion Experience
http://www.ICAdventures.com

Williwaw Adventures
http://www.williwawadventures.com

Youth for Understanding USA
http://www.yfu-usa.org

China Adventure and Explore Africa
http://www.msu.edu/user/gifted

American Trails West European Adventures
http://www.atwteentours.com

FALCON (Chinese or Japanese Language Concentration)
http://lrc.cornell.edu/falcon/index.html

Summer Program for High School Students
http://www.ce.columbia.edu/hs

Summer Study at The Sorbonne in Paris and The Barcelona Experience
http://www.summerstudy.com/index.cfm

Westcoast Connection Teen Travel Experiences
http://www.westcoastconnection.com

Longacre Expeditions
http://www.longacreexpeditions.com

Amigos de las Américas
http://www.amigoslink.org

Gap Year Advisory Services and Transitions Abroad Magazine
http://www.transitionsabroad.com/listings/study/teen/advisoryservices.shtml

Service Learning in Paris
http://www.study-serve.org

Volunteers For Peace (VFP)
http://www.vfp.org

Pacific Village Institute
http://www.pacificvillage.org

National Outdoor Leadership School (NOLS)
http://www.nols.edu

American Study Associates
http://www.asaprograms.com/home/asa_home.asp

University of Dallas Summer Programs Abroad
http://www.udallas.edu/travel/hs.cfm

should be a part of writing the story of you and should be consistent with your overall goals.

The number of gap year programs and consultants is on the increase and shouldn't be difficult to find. It's far better to take a year off than to enter a professional field and suddenly realize that you are in the wrong place. This happens to adults who, all too often, say that they ended up in their profession because of someone else's expectations or that they simply drifted into it without pausing to think whether they really loved their work. Many students get into a college and attend for 2 or more years before deciding that they are in the wrong place. This is not because the college has changed. Rather, it is because the student has changed and needs a different environment. However, transferring to a different school may cost some earned credit hours because your new school does not have to accept all of your credits. If you can structure your summers as one method to explore academic subjects and career paths, you are less likely to fall into the wrong school or wrong career trap.

If a college that you want to attend has accepted you for admission, taking a gap year requires deferral. Here is how that works: To defer, you will put down an enrollment deposit by May 1 (or thereafter if you are admitted off of a waiting list). Then, you will ask the college, in writing, to hold your place while you defer admission, usually for a full year but sometimes only for a semester.

If you did not apply to any colleges, were not admitted to any, or were admitted only to colleges in which you have no interest, then you are considering a different track: a real gap year during which you will apply (or reapply) to a full list of colleges while pursuing activities that interest you and that will improve your chances of getting in.

If you are taking time off from school, you may want to look at the "time out" programs included in Table 2.

ACADEMIC PROGRAMS

Choosing an academic program requires students to look closely at their planned 4-year high school program and their own strengths and weaknesses. As stated earlier, students who choose to accelerate by taking an out-of-school course may find themselves in the unenviable position of repeating that course in school at a much slower pace because the high school will not acknowledge the student's acceleration and mastery. Before you enroll in an academic course for which you want school credit and advanced placement, make sure that your school will cooperate. If you take an Advanced Placement course in a summer program, make sure that you take the AP test and that your score is recorded on your transcript. If you did not take the AP test, investigate taking the test when your school gives it. Enrichment courses like ancient Greek or Existentialism do not cause problems with schools because there is no expectation of school credit. Teenagers take enrichment courses because they are interested in exploring a topic that is not normally taught in their middle or high school and are looking for a fast-paced, intense experience.

Learning style (i.e., the way you learn, including your preferred learning environment) should be a significant factor when choosing an academic course (Olszewski-Kubilius, 2007). Students who are highly organized, have strong study skills, and can work independently usually can handle an intensive accelerated course that moves quickly. Students who tend to be focused in one specific talent area may be more comfortable studying a single subject in great depth. The pace is slower, but no less intense. Some students do not have intellectual peers in their home school district and enroll in courses for social, as well as academic, reasons. These students may want to sample courses by taking one class in the morning and a different class in the afternoon. The courses may or may not appear on the student's transcript so make sure that documentation is in your portfolio that eventually will go to the colleges to which you apply.

You'll want to keep several other considerations in mind as you choose an academic program, including:

- *Location*: If you are not accustomed to the part of the country where classes are located, ask the program director if you can speak with previous attendees. Preparing yourself for the weather in a different part of the country may seem trivial now, but inclement weather without proper clothing can be a real downer. You will also want to prepare yourself to navigate the area on your own by consulting maps (and travel guides if the program is overseas or in a big city, like New York City) and finding out information about public transportation in the area.

- *Class Size*: Are you comfortable in a lecture hall with 800 other students or do you need a small class? Check with the program director or previous attendees to find out the class size and if it is suitable to your learning preferences. If you are easily distracted, avoid the lecture hall or sit in the front row.

- *Recreation*: Do other teens bring bikes? What else might you need? Should teens leave electronic gadgets such as iPods at home? Find out if the program offers additional outings on weekends and if there is an extra cost to participate in such outings.

- *Additional Qualifications*: Some programs require students to have previous experience or special qualifications. For example, some marine programs require students to have a valid SCUBA certification and strong swimming ability. Some require students to have strong research skills.

TABLE 2:
GAP YEAR PROGRAMS TO CONSIDER

SIENA SOJOURN
3030 Bridgeway, Suite 233
Sausalito, CA 94965
PHONE: 415-332-1831
FAX: 415-332-6205
E-MAIL: siena@sojournsabroad.org
WEB SITE: http://www.sienasojourn.com

TIME OUT ADVENTURES
CONTACT: David Denman
3030 Bridgeway Avenue, #233
Sausalito, CA 94965
PHONE: 415-332-1831
FAX: 415-332-6205
E-MAIL: TimeODave@aol.com
WEB SITE: http://www.timeoutadventures.org
DESCRIPTION: Both Siena Sojourn and Time Out Adventures are structured for students who want to travel between high school and college. Time Out Adventures designs learning opportunities for young people providing experiences in group travel, community involvement, and personal development.

THE CENTER FOR INTERIM PROGRAMS
195 Nassau St., Second Floor, Ste. 5
Princeton, NJ 08542
PHONE: 609-683-4300
FAX: 609-683-4309
WEB SITE: http://www.interimprograms.com
DESCRIPTION: This is a service that enables people to pursue structured alternatives to formal education by matching their clients' interests with more than 5,000 internships, volunteer positions, apprenticeships, cultural studies programs, and more worldwide to create "time off" that can give a new direction, sharpen hazy career goals, rejuvenate those on the verge of burnout, and provide a break to students between high school and college or those already in college.

TAKING OFF

CONTACT: Gail Reardon, Director
12 Marlborough Street
Boston, MA 02116 USA
PHONE: 617-424-1606
FAX: 617-344-0481 (fax)
E-MAIL: takingoff@takingoff.net
WEB SITE: http://www.takingoff.net/public_html/pages/lure.htm
DESCRIPTION: This is a counseling and placement service for gap year students, ages 16–25. The director says that you don't have to be rich to take a gap year. Many people cover expenses by working, economizing and plain old roughing it. A lot of internships pay at least a little money. Taking Off works closely with students to maximize their time and experience.

WHERE YOU HEADED

CONTACT: Robert P. Gilpin
P.O. Box 503
Milton, MA 02186
PHONE: 617-698-8977
E-MAIL: info@whereyouheaded.com
WEB SITE: http://whereyouheaded.com/home1.asp
DESCRIPTION: Where You Headed is part counseling, part membership organization, and part database. Membership includes access to a database of thousands of program opportunities along with access to the counseling staff. They also offer college application assistance, preparing students for the various elements of the college application process.

DYNAMY INTERNSHIP YEAR

CONTACT: Mr. Greg Cappello, Director of Admission
Dynamy Admissions Dept.
27 Sever Street
Worcester MA 01609
PHONE: 508-755-2571 ext. 18
FAX: 508-755-4692
E-MAIL: admissions@dynamy.org
WEB SITE: http://www.dynamy.org
DESCRIPTION: Dynamy, Inc. is a not-for-profit experiential educational organization founded in 1969. It is the oldest and only residential internship program in the country. Its mission is to offer young people, ages 17–22, a gap year opportunity like no other. Dynamy programs integrate independent city apartment living with mentored internships, personal and college/career advising, urban and wilderness leadership opportunities, and the company of an incredible group of peers.

Check with the program to see if any prerequisites are required, and if so, how you can go about arranging the completion of these requirements.

- *Staff to Student Ratio*: Check out the number of faculty or teachers per student, especially if you expect to be doing research. If there are 20 students per teacher, don't expect a lot of one-on-one mentoring. The ratio is particularly important if you are doing field research (e.g., an archeology site) and recording scientific observations. Speak with previous attendees and ask what to expect.

- *Staff Qualifications*: Before you commit to a research program, verify the seriousness of the project. Are the leaders affiliated with a university or well-established research facility? Have scientists published earlier work in the topic? Working with a research scientist in a laboratory is a remarkable opportunity, especially if you will be allowed to publish. The experience is likely to give you credibility when you apply to colleges. At the very least, it will give you some credentials in the field. Make sure you ask the researchers you work with for a letter of recommendation that can accompany your college application. If you wait until you are filling out applications, the researchers' memory of you may not be fresh.

FINE AND PERFORMING ARTS

Fine and performing arts is a broad category that covers a multitude of talent areas including studio, performing, theater and visual arts, dance, music, and so forth. They all have at least one thing in common—because of school district budget cutbacks few young students are exposed to the arts through their schools. In many schools, all forms of the arts have quietly disappeared from school curricula. Until a few years ago, a school band was integral to elementary and middle schools. Students learned to read music while learning to play an instrument. Today, school art and music classes are no longer a given. School policymakers say that they had to choose between an arts teacher or a teacher who can teach science, math, social studies, or language arts. By implication, the arts have become something that children can do if their parents have the money to pay for it and if it's important to the family.

We live in a modern world where art and music are digitized, synthesized, and downloaded, and it's easier to find a computer camp than a summer arts program. Some states (e.g., North and South Carolina) host year-round programs for students who can qualify. Summer programs are offered to middle and high school students. Some programs are free and others are quite expensive. Some programs are part of a national system of Governor's Schools providing intensive high-quality experiences focusing on diverse areas of art or science. Many states offer a residential Governor's School program only to students who are between their junior and senior years. Some are open to any state or out-of-state resident who can pay the cost of the program. Specific criteria for selection of students differ, depending on the State. For more information, including a list of schools with contact information, visit the Web site for the National Conference for Governor's Schools at http://ncogs.org/home.

Many young students who take summer classes in the arts are experimenting. That's one of the joys of summer—you can try out different areas to see if you have talent, to see if you want to spend more time acquiring expertise, or just for the exposure. If that sounds like you, you may be able to find a suitable arts program in the enrichment programs listed in this book. For example, one noncompetitive program, Oxbow Summer Art Camp in California, offers arts immersion for students ages 14–17. If you are at a higher level of expertise, ask your teachers about summer programs. During the summer, many private teachers teach at well-known institutes such as Tanglewood in Massachusetts and have connections to a wide variety of resources. If you are interested in performing arts, check your local newspaper for auditions and casting calls.

Here are a few tips to guide your choices:

- *Program Placement*: Your selected program should match your level of experience and accomplishment. This is less of a problem if the program requires auditions.

- *Quality of Faculty/Teachers*: Does the program use their advanced students as summer teachers or will you be working with artists who are fine teachers?

- *Career Opportunities*: If you are an advanced student, will the program or faculty open some doors for you?

If you are a serious artist, there are a host of summer programs with some scholarships available. Many universities and colleges are known for their summer arts programs. For example, North Carolina, New York, Connecticut, Ohio, and Oregon all have schools with fine reputations. Innerspark, the California state school for the arts, offers a talented group of high school students intensive training from professionals in music, theatre, video and film, visual arts, dance, and creative writing. Admission is competitive. Because it is a summer program, directors can hire a variety of well-known teachers who return to their own schools during winter sessions. This is one of the advantages of attending a summer program. Students are able to study with a variety of teachers, each with his or her area of expertise, and gain a different perspective from each. Needless to say, studying with a variety of people shows college admission faculty that you are committed to the arts. Make sure you get letters of recommendation from everyone who can speak to your work, even if you are not yet ready to apply to colleges.

People who study intensively may find that they need to take an "incubation" break during the summer. Sometimes it's healthier to sit by a lake watching nothing in particular. For dancers, it's an opportunity to rest one's body. For visual and similar creative artists, a short break can be a catalyst for renewed energy and motivation.

SERVICE LEARNING

Another option for summer involvement is service learning. Service learning has been defined in many ways, but the core of its definition lies in connecting experiential learning (learning by doing) with community service. Service learning is a teaching and learning strategy that integrates meaningful community service with instruction and reflection to enrich the learning experience, teach civic responsibility, and strengthen communities. Young people apply academic skills to solving real-world issues, linking established learning objectives with genuine needs. They lead the process, with adults as partners, applying critical thinking and problem-solving skills to concerns such as hunger, pollution, and diversity.

Service learning is different from volunteering or internships because of its structure and connection to academics. Groups are well organized and led by adults in the field. Students may earn community service hours, but if earning service hours is the primary goal, you might consider an activity that is less challenging, such as reading to senior citizens who have lost their sight. Benefits of service learning for students include increased academic skills in relevant subjects (e.g., grammar, math, computers); an enhanced sense of confidence, self-efficacy, perseverance, and responsibility; and new perspectives on political, interpersonal, or occupational relationships (Terry, 2000). Researchers suggest that students benefit from service learning because it provides them with challenging extended curricula that stimulate advanced critical thinking skills, higher level thinking processes, and problem-solving abilities.

Examples of service learning projects are available at the following Web sites:
- The National Service-Learning Clearinghouse (http://www.servicelearning.org)
- National Youth Leadership Council (http://www.nylc.org)
- National Association of Student Councils (http://www.nasc.us/s_nasc/sec.asp?CID=442&DID=47824)

YOUTH LEADERSHIP PROGRAMS

Leadership camps provide young people with memories that last a lifetime, but they also have a very practical and expanding role. These camp experiences provide teens with the opportunity to develop knowledge, skills, and attitudes associated with socially responsible leadership. Students say that program activities inspire, encourage, and develop leadership skills. If you are looking for a leadership program, look beyond the general language into "how" they do this. Do they just talk about the merits of developing leadership skills? Or do they say specifically what attendees can expect in the way of courses? As an example, look at Brown University's Pre-College Leadership Institute at http://brown.edu/Administration/Continuing_Studies/pc/leadership/index.php. The courses are clearly stated, as is the way Brown extends learning into the general community.

STATEWIDE LEADERSHIP EXPERIENCES

Many states nominate students to attend state leadership programs through their Governor's Schools. The other well-known programs are Boys and Girls State, and the Hugh O'Brien Youth Foundation (HOBY). Boys State and Girls State are summer leadership and citizenship programs sponsored by the American Legion and the American Legion Auxiliary for high school students between their junior and senior years. Boys and Girls State programs are held in each of the U.S. states (excluding Hawaii), usually on a college campus within that state. Typically, students are nominated by an American Legion post, which pays the student's tuition.

Thousands of high school students will attend HOBY (http://www.hoby.org) programs each year, including Community Leadership Workshops (CLeW), U.S. State Leadership Seminars, and the World Leadership Congress. CLeW is a one-day introductory HOBY leadership session for high school freshmen. Leadership Seminars are designed for high school sophomores to recognize their leadership talents and apply them in becoming effective, ethical leaders in their home, schools, workplace, and community. The World Leadership Congress, the next level of leadership training, is a weeklong intensive educational program held every summer in Washington, D.C.

The National Association of Secondary School Principals sponsors summer leadership camps in many states. They also publish *Leadership for Student Activities*, a monthly magazine for members of the National Association of Student Councils, the National Honor Society, and the National Junior Honor Society. Each month during the school year, *Leadership for Student Activities* focuses on a topic of interest to student leaders in middle and high school and their advisers.

The National Association of Student Councils promotes and provides leadership development opportunities to prepare and empower student leaders to serve their schools and communities. For specific information on leadership camps in your area, contact your state branch of this organization.

VOLUNTEER PROGRAMS

Volunteer programs require that you provide services to help others without the intention of a monetary reward, complete tasks for which you receive minimal payment, or join programs in which you pay to participate in helping others. If you are volunteering outside the United States, you should plan on a significant expense. If you want to volunteer in your community, start by asking yourself, "What's in my backyard?" Some organizations won't take volunteers because they can't train them or because their insurance won't cover volunteers. But, there are enough places that welcome volunteers, so keep asking if you are interested in a particular venue or career field. The people you help will appreciate your efforts.

Teens usually volunteer for several reasons: to fulfill community service obligations, because of a belief in a cause bigger than oneself, to gain credentials or experience in a specific field, to explore career options, or because nothing else has an appeal. To truly explore career goals, volunteers must plan on participating in a program for a considerable length of time so you can see all of the aspects and talk to a lot of people about educational choices or other areas. Be prepared to ask, "What did you do that you are very glad you did" and "What did you do that you haven't needed?" There is so much variance among programs that, again, there are only a few considerations that cross programs.

When looking for volunteer programs, start by asking your school counselors and teachers. Then use the Web to find community directories of programs that have been certified or accredited by an outside agency. Look for programs in your backyard like the American Red Cross, local hospitals, your city's Department of Parks and Recreation, senior citizen assisted living facilities, Big Brothers Big Sisters, or the YMCA. Forbes magazine publishes a list of opportunities (http://www.forbes.com) in cooperation with VolunteerMatch (http://www.volunteermatch.org). USA Today (http://www.usatoday.com) also publishes an annual list of volunteer organizations.

INTERNSHIPS

An internship offers you an opportunity to test your interest in an area before you make a commitment to further study or career preparation. Some programs let you try out what it is like to work in a supervised position all day, day after day, in a particular field. The word *intern* often refers to a variety of activities in which a person receives firsthand experience in a field, usually for minimum or no pay, under the direct guidance and supervision of a professional. Finding a position takes time because the number of internships in any one firm or agency is very limited. You may be able to find an internship through your high school guidance department or City Council. Contacting the trade association in your field of interest can lead to an internship, as well as a lot of contacts. There is usually a trade association for every field. *Imagine*, a student magazine published by the Center for Talented Youth at Johns Hopkins University, includes a column in every issue spotlighting a career. The column, "Exploring Career Options," usually includes an interview with someone in the field, as well as information on the required education, the job outlook, salary range, and resources for more information. They also include some information on internships.

The areas of service learning, community service, internships, and volunteerism intersect one another at different junctions. When you are looking for this type of activity, especially on the Internet, be aware that the terms mean different things to different people. Be creative in your search when looking for these types of programs.

Now that you know a little about each of the types of programs available, you'll want to decide which interests you most and move on to the next step: finding and selecting the right program for you.

CHAPTER 4

BUT, HOW DO I FIND A PROGRAM?

Once you've considered what kind of program you might be interested in, it's time to start looking for opportunities. You'll want to make sure that you peruse the programs in this book, but also ask your guidance counselor, teachers, and friends for suggestions. Sometimes, little-known programs in your community offer fabulous experiences.

FINDING AND CHOOSING A SUMMER PROGRAM

This book offers more than 200 programs, selected from a much larger group, whose organizers said their programs meet the needs of college-bound youth. The program you choose should be a good match for your needs. For example, if you are not accustomed to hiking, a rugged trek in Mongolia probably is not the program for you. If you are afraid of snakes, you may want to avoid the Southeast Asian rainforest. Some consultants believe that there are no bad programs, just bad fits.

Finding appropriate programs depends on the usual things such as location and cost. Your family might want some input on your choice of activity, especially if they are helping to pay for a program or if they are going to transport you. If you find that you are interested in everything, look at your own strengths and interests. Is there any area where you want to learn more? The following questions might help in your evaluation (Berger, 2006; Ware, 1990):

- What are your academic and social strengths?

- What academic or social weaknesses might you have that can be addressed in a summer program?

- What *new* opportunities (academics, recreational and/or social) would benefit or better prepare you for the future? What do *you* want to do?

- If you are involved in an activity in school, is there a summer experience where you can learn more about that activity?

- What are the criteria for acceptance to a program you are considering? If you want something academic, you need to plan at least 6 months in advance. You may need to take the PSAT or some other test to be eligible to participate.

- Do you have any health issues? (If you are horribly allergic to bees or plants, you may want to choose a program that keeps you away from wildlife.)

Some other nonacademic questions your parents should ask:

- How is the food? Does the program provide for special diets?

- What type of social activities does the program provide?

- Where will the student get medical care, if necessary? If a student requires medication, who will dispense it? Is a physician on call or on site each date? What are the credentials of people who staff the infirmary? How far is the nearest hospital? What type of insurance does the camp offer in case a camper gets hurt?

- If a program stresses "communing with nature," is it really a nature camp or is it a regular program with outside activities?

- Summer is a great time to "unplug," to get away from electronics for a while. If the cell phone is home, how do campers contact their families? Are students allowed to send e-mail messages and are there rules governing the use of e-mail? Be sure to ask the program if campers have access to electronic games, computers, and video devices.

When you start to research summer opportunities, the following areas are important for you and your family to keep in mind.

- *Length*: Programs vary from 1 to 10 weeks. Length affects the skill level that can be reached and the overall cost.

- *Age range*: Determine the age range of participants and the way they are grouped to know whether a camper will be with peers or will be one of the oldest or youngest members.

- *Requirements*: In some types of programs, especially in academics and music, the requirements for application can provide a clue to what one can expect. For example, a music program that requires a tape or audition may involve more difficult orchestral music than a program that takes anyone who has had one year of lessons.

- *Size*: The overall number of participants, as well as the size of activity or study groups, affects the atmosphere of a program and the kinds of activities that are possible.

- *Individual attention*: Closely related to size is the ratio of leaders or teachers to participants. The lower the ratio, the more individual attention one can expect.

- *Leadership*: There is not one ideal background of a leader or teacher. They include professionals, experienced volunteers, and teachers at all levels: college faculty, public and private school teachers, and undergraduate teaching assistants. The common qualities that make them appropriate are experience in their field, experience and pleasure in working with young people, and the flexibility and desire to be in a summer program setting.

- *Depth of experience*: Ask the staff and previous participants for specific examples of the activities and the skill level they develop to judge whether the program is an appropriate match for your abilities and goals.

- *Credit or not-for-credit courses*: A program's approach to credit is an integral part of its philosophy. Programs that do not grant credit want to encourage students to pursue a topic at length without being concerned about grades. Credit-granting programs view grades as a normal part of an academic experience.

- *Facilities and equipment*: The quality of the facilities and the amount of equipment impact the level of involvement. One computer for every two participants allows more work time than one computer for five participants. This also applies to laboratory, art, drama, music, and sports equipment.

- *Schedule*: Does the participant want to have every minute scheduled, or does he or she prefer a more relaxed pace that includes unscheduled free time?

- *Recreation*: To what extent are athletics or other recreational activities such as arts or drama offered or required? Some organizations require an hour or two of individual or team sports daily. Others view activities as optional.

- *Social activities*: Most programs plan informal group activities for participants to get to know one another. A few programs leave this up to the students.

- *Safety*: In all programs safety is of paramount importance. Ask about the training and qualifications of the instructors, the certifications or inspections the program has passed, and the provisions that are made for safety.

DIRECTORIES

This book is an example of the many directories of summer programs that exist. Many of the talent search programs publish directories that list camps and programs. Typically, someone has culled Web sites and categorized them, so the tedious work has been done for you. Before you start searching, go to the Web site of your state gifted advocacy group. You will find a list at http://www.hoagiesgifted.org/regional_orgs.htm#usa. Many of these groups offer directories or lists of programs on their Web sites. They may not endorse the programs but you may be able to contact the group and ask if anyone has direct experience with a program that interests you. Major search engines like Google and Yahoo also have directories of summer programs. Other resources for directories can be found in Table 3.

INDEPENDENT CONSULTANTS

One of the safest and most efficient ways of finding a summer program is to use a private licensed independent consultant. These consultants often visit the programs while they are in session and can tell you what to expect. If you need help finding a consultant, contact the Independent Educational Consultants Association (http://www.educationalconsulting.org/counselors_summer.html). IECA member consultants counsel students and their families in the selection of educational programs, based on the student's individual needs and talents. The fee varies with the counselor's expertise and geographical area.

Many communities have camp advisors or summer enrichment fairs. Camp advisors frequently do not charge families; rather, they charge the programs to whom they refer clients. This means that you may not hear about small programs that do not want to pay camp advisor fees. If you live in a community where there is a gifted advocacy group, find out if they publish a list of summer programs

---

RESOURCES AND DIRECTORIES FOR SUMMER OPPORTUNITIES

NATIONAL ASSOCIATION FOR GIFTED CHILDREN RESOURCE DIRECTORY
http://www.nagc.org/resourcedirectory.aspx

GUIDE TO EDUCATIONAL PROGRAMS
Duke University
http://www.tip.duke.edu

SUMMER OPPORTUNITIES FOR KIDS AND TEENAGERS
http://www.petersons.com/books/summeropportunitieskidsteens.asp

EDUCATIONAL PROGRAM GUIDE
Midwest Academic Talent Search
http://www.ctd.northwestern.edu/mats

IMAGINE: OPPORTUNITIES AND RESOURCES
FOR ACADEMICALLY TALENTED YOUTH
Johns Hopkins University
http://cty.jhu.edu/imagine

INSTITUTE FOR EDUCATIONAL ADVANCEMENT (IEA)
http://www.educationaladvancement.org

---

or sponsor a summer enrichment fair. Look for fairs near your home by visiting http://www.summercampfair.net or call Summer Solutions at 1-800-729-7295 or e-mail info@summercampfair.net. Another excellent resource is the American Camping Association. Its Web site offers a "Find a Camp" tool. Go to http://www.acacamp.org and select "Parents and Families: Find a Camp."

Several other Web sites are available for searching out appropriate programs, including:

- Great Summers, which provides personalized search mechanisms for grade 8–11 programs at http://www.greatsummers.org;

- Thomson and Peterson's Guide, which has an extensive listing of academic programs, travel programs, and summer jobs at http://www.petersons.com/summerop;

- Camp Page, which provides links to accredited U.S. and Canadian summer camps and jobs at http://www.camppage.com; and

- Teen Ink, whose list (http://teenink.com/Summer) runs the gamut from short-term work-related jobs, to writing and engineering camps, to those located on university campuses, ships, and overseas.

Some summer opportunities are designed to attract bright teens to a career field. For example, NASA's Summer High School Apprenticeship Research Program, or SHARP, at the Marshall Space Flight Center in Huntsville, AL, selects students for a 8-week program based on their aptitude for, and interest in, science and engineering careers. Supervised by mentors, the students conduct research, analyze data, develop their oral and written communications, and polish their computer and leadership skills.

If you have special needs, contact your advocacy group and ask about camps. For example, Camp AZDA is one of many camps across the U.S. that is designed for kids with diabetes and run by the American Diabetes Association. (Visit http://www.diabetes.org to find a diabetes camp near you.)

PAYING FOR PROGRAMS

Before selecting and applying to a summer program, discuss the costs of summer programs with your parents or guardians. Ask your parents for a budget of how much money they are willing and able to spend on a summer program. Make sure that when you look for programs, you don't discount programs with little or no fees attached. Sometimes, the best summer programs are those run by your local university or Parks Department for a minimal fee. Sometimes, summer opportunities can be as simple as volunteering at your local church, school, hospital, museum, or zoo, or working as an unpaid intern in your county or city offices. In this case, you'll only need to set aside enough money for your transportation to and from your position. Assuming that you have already looked at no-cost programs, the first and most obvious strategy is to ask the program you want to attend for a scholarship. Some programs have scholarship money set aside for students who cannot afford the program.

There are two types of financial aid: merit based and need based. Merit-based funds are very competitive but always worth trying for. The Davidson Institute (http://www.davidsonfellows.org) has resources for merit-based aid, as does The Jack Kent Cooke Foundation (http://www.jackkentcookefoundation.org), which is gaining a reputation as a good source for aid. Need-based funds are usually based on your family income and generally require that your family submit their most recent tax statement. Check the American Camp Association Web site (http://www.acacamps.org) for information on some need-based programs. For example, one such program is the Break-Aways Partnerships for Year-Round Learning that provides New York City Board of Education (NYCBOE) school children with an opportunity to attend summer camp while simultaneously combating summer learning loss.

Students should contact your state gifted association and local parent groups, which often have merit-based and need-based funds set aside to help gifted or talented children and teens attend summer programs. State gifted associations are listed on the National Association for Gifted Children Web site (http://www.nagc.org). Another option is to check with your school's PTA or PTO, and local organizations like the American Legion, Junior League, religious groups, or other volunteer fraternal and sororal organizations. Such community groups set aside money to help students in need. By contacting these organizations, you may find opportunities for scholarships or help for minor expenses like equipment, travel, or books. If you are persuasive, you may even be able to convince a local business to pay for a summer program in exchange for work during the winter or some other commodity. Check with your local Chamber of Commerce for information.

If you can't find money donated by local or state organizations or businesses, don't fret. You can always organize your own fund-raising possibilities, by asking neighbors if you can do yard or housework for them in exchange for a donation. Garage sales, bake sales, and car washes are all effective ways for several students to pitch in to help raise money for summer programs that will be split among the group. Babysitting for friends and family, providing care for elderly family members, designing Web sites, or even taking on a part-time job on the weekends during the school year and up to the point when you leave for your summer program are all viable options of raising the money you plan to spend during your summer program.

The more care you take in seeking the answers to large and small questions, the greater probability of success in finding an appropriate and valuable summer pursuit. Whatever you decide to do, have a great summer!

REFERENCES

American Camp Association (2005). *Directions: Youth development outcomes of the camp experience.* Retrieved May 1, 2007 from http://www.acacamps.org/research/marsh/mtreviewlit.php.

Berger, S., (2006). *College planning for gifted students: Choosing and getting into the right college.* Waco, TX: Prufrock Press.

Davidson, J. & Davidson, B. (2004). *Genius denied: How to stop wasting our brightest young minds.* NY: Simon & Schuster.

Ellis, D. (2002). *Becoming a master student* (10th ed.). Boston: Houghton Mifflin.

How can I get a job in oceanography, especially at the Woods Hole Oceanographic Institution? (2004). Retrieved June 13, 2007, from http://www.whoi.edu/info/careers.html

Mendelsohn, D., Moshan, M., & Shapiro, M. (2006). *Rock the SAT.* Columbus, OH: McGraw-Hill.

Olszewski-Kubilius, P. (2007). The role of summer programs in developing the talents of gifted students. In J. L. VanTassel-Baska (Ed.), *Serving gifted learners beyond the traditional classroom* (pp. 13–32). Waco, TX: Prufrock Press.

Terry, A.W. (2000). An early glimpse: Service learning from an adolescent perspective. *Journal of Secondary Gifted Education, 11*(3), 115–35.

Ware, C. (1990). *Discovering interests and talents through summer experiences.* Retrieved May 10, 2007, from: http://www.ericdigests.org/pre-9216/talents.htm (ERIC Document Reproduction Service No. ED321496)

What is TASP? (n.d.). Retrieved June 13, 2007, from http://www.tellurideassociation.org/tasp1.html

SUMMER PROGRAM DIRECTORY

Program:	**Engineering Summer Camp (ESC)**
Contact:	Robin Douglass, Summer Camp Coordinator
Address:	The University of Alabama in Huntsville College of Engineering EB 102 Huntsville, AL 35899
Phone:	256-824-3590
Fax:	256-824-6843
E-mail:	douglar@uah.edu; esc@eng.uah.edu
Web site:	http://www.eng.uah.edu/camp
Program Type:	Math, Sciences, Engineering, and Computer Science/Technology
Grade/Age Levels:	Rising grades 11–12
Description:	Engineering Summer Camp (ESC) is a weeklong day camp designed for high school students interested in learning about the various fields of engineering.

Program:	**PreFreshman in Computer Science Summer Program (PREFICS)**
Contact:	Ms. Cassandra Thomas, Program Coordinator, PREFICS
Address:	Tuskegee University Computer Science Department Wilcox E Tuskegee, AL 36088
Phone:	334-727-8587; 334-727-8593
E-mail:	cthomas@tuskegee.edu
Web site:	http://www.tuskegee.edu/Global/category.asp?C=35313
Program Type:	Math, Sciences, Engineering, and Computer Science/Technology
Grade/Age Levels:	Grades 13–20
Description:	An 8-week summer program for high school graduates. Selected students will have the opportunity to earn up to seven credit hours in college level mathematics and computer science. These courses will develop and strengthen the students' problem solving and critical reasoning skills—the foundation of computer science.

Program:	**Summer Y.E.S.**
Contact:	Kristy Farmer, Summer Program Director
Address:	Auburn University 131 Sciences Center Classroom Building College of Sciences and Mathematics Auburn, AL 36849
Phone:	334-844-7449
Fax:	334-844-5740
E-mail:	farmekr@auburn.edu
Web site:	http://www.auburn.edu/academic/science_math/ cosam/outreach/programs/summeryes/index.htm
Program Type:	Academic Enrichment
Grade/Age Levels:	Rising grades 6–9
Description:	Summer Y.E.S. (Youth Experiences in Science), a program sponsored and hosted by the AU College of Sciences and Mathematics, offers a variety of mini-courses in science and math taught by university faculty and certified science teachers that are fun, challenging, and sure to keep your child talking about science long after summer is over!

Activities have included:

- *Krashers I and II:* Build a car that safely carries an egg through a 30 mph crash.
- *Medical Technology and Forensics:* Use forensic technology to solve a crime.
- *Snakes and Lizards oh My!:* Learn about different reptiles and amphibians that live all around us.
- *Silly Putty Science:* Create and analyze Silly Putty and other slimy, gooey concoctions.

Program:	Alaska Native Tribal Health Consortium Summer Internship
Address:	Alaska Native Tribal Health Consortium 4000 Ambassador Dr. Anchorage, AK 99508
Phone:	907-729-1900
Fax:	907-729-1901
Web site:	http://www.anthc.org
Program Type:	Internships/Paid Positions
Grade/Age Levels:	Grades 9 and up
Description:	The Alaska Native Tribal Health Consortium awards approximately 25 9-week paid summer internships to high school and undergraduate students who are Alaska Native or American Indian permanent Alaska residents. Students receive work experience in a range of medical professions and support services including computer technology, engineering, health records, and human resources.

ALASKA

Program:	**A Summer of Excellence**
Address:	The University of Arizona The Honors College P.O. Box 210006 Tucson, AZ 85721-0006
Phone:	520-621-6901
Fax:	520-621-8655
E-mail:	soe@email.arizona.edu
Web site:	http://www.soe.honors.arizona.edu
Program Type:	Academic Enrichment
Grade/Age Levels:	Grades 10–12
Description:	The University of Arizona's premier residential summer program for academically talented high school students is open to both Arizona residents and out of state students. A precollege program, A Summer of Excellence provides high school students with a fun and intellectually challenging summer. Students can earn transferable college credit and participate in extracurricular activities through the program.

ARIZONA

Program:	**Astronomy Camp for Teens**
Contact:	Dr. Donald McCarthy, Jr., Astronomer
Address:	University of Arizona Alumni Association Steward Observatory 933 N. Cherry Ave. Tucson, AZ 85721
Phone:	520-621-4079
Fax:	520-621-9843
E-mail:	dmccarthy@as.arizona.edu
Web site:	http://www.astronomycamp.org
Program Type:	Math, Sciences, Engineering, & Computer Science/Technology
Grade/Age Levels:	Ages 13–19
Description:	Astronomy Camps are immersion adventures in doing science. Participants become astronomers operating large telescopes (12, 20, 40, 60, 61-inch diameters), interacting with leading scientists, and interpreting their own scientific observations. The camps are held in the "Sky Island" environment of Mt. Lemmon Observatory (9200 feet). Daytime activities include solar observing, construction projects, interactive talks, inquiry-based activities led by astronomers and educators, and tours of the UA Mirror Lab and other facilities.

ARIZONA

Program:	**American Intercultural Student Exchange**
Contact:	Ms. Judy Scott, President
Address:	American Intercultural Student Exchange 707 Lake Hall Road Lake Village, AR 71653
Phone:	800-SIBLING
Fax:	870-265-5001
E-mail:	pscott@aise.com
Web site:	http://www.aise.com
Program Type:	Gap Year/Study Abroad/International Travel
Grade/Age Levels:	Ages 15–18
Description:	American Intercultural Student Exchange is a nonprofit foundation dedicated to building international relations among students. American students have the opportunity to become exchange students in an overseas household and school, and students from other countries are matched with host families and schools in the U.S. The program serves more than 4,000 students and families each year and offers both school-year and summer exchange options.

Program:	University of Arkansas Summer Institute for Gifted & Talented Scholars
Contact:	Keith Brink, Director of Gifted & Talented Programs
Address:	200 Hotz Hall Fayetteville, AR 72701
Phone:	479-575-3553; 866-625-9247
E-mail:	kbrink@uark.edu
Web site:	http://gtscholars.uark.edu/home.php
Program Type:	Academic Enrichment
Grade/Age Levels:	Grades K–12
Description:	*Summer Institute for Gifted & Talented Scholars* provides an intensive 3-week residential experience for students completing the seventh, eighth, and ninth grades with exceptional academic ability. Academic areas include mathematics, science, computer science, international affairs, architecture, fine arts, engineering, composition, and literature. *The Gifted and Talented Scholars Program* serves outstanding students in grades 6–12. *The Summer Laureate University for Youth* (SLUFY), for grades K–7, is an educational program that provides unique learning experiences for students to explore and expand their talents and abilities in a university environment. The summer program offers a variety of classes.

ARKANSAS

Program:	**Asian American Journalists Association (AAJA) J Camp**
Contact:	Ms. Kimberly Mizuhara, Student Programs Coordinator
Address:	J Camp Asian American Journalists Association 1182 Market St., Ste. 320 San Francisco, CA 94102
Phone:	415-346-2051
Fax:	415-346-6343
E-mail:	programs@aaja.org
Web site:	http://www.aaja.org/programs/for_students/j_camp
Program Type:	Academic Enrichment
Grade/Age Levels:	Grades 9–11
Description:	J Camp is a multicultural journalism program for talented high school students. This free training camp brings together a multicultural group of talented high school students from across the nation for 6 days of intensive journalism training.

Program:	**California College of the Arts Pre-College Program**
Contact:	Robin Strawbridge, Pre-College Program Coordinator
Address:	California College of the Arts 1111 Eighth Street San Francisco, CA 94107-2247
Phone:	415-703-9500; 800-447-1ART
E-mail:	info@cca.edu
Web site:	http://www.cca.edu
Program Type:	Fine, Performing, and Visual Arts; Academic Enrichment
Grade/Age Levels:	Grades 6–12
Description:	The Pre-College Program at California College of the Arts provides an opportunity for high school students to study art or creative writing in an art school setting while earning three college credits. The program also enables participants to develop strong portfolio pieces for college admissions. The three programs have different admission requirements. Visit Web site for application and housing details. During the summer, the college also offers *Summer Atelier* (two 3-week sessions) for students who have completed their freshman year of high school, as well as a *Young Artist Studio Program* designed for students who have completed the sixth, seventh, or eighth grade.

CALIFORNIA

Program:	**California Polytechnic University Architecture Summer Career Workshop**
Contact:	Mr. Michael Lucas, Associate Professor, Workshop Director
Address:	Architecture Summer Career Workshop California Polytechnic University, San Luis Obispo Architecture Department/College of Continuing Education San Luis Obispo, CA 93407
Phone:	805-756-1790
E-mail:	mlucas@calpoly.edu
Web site:	http://www.arch.calpoly.edu/events
Program Type:	Academic Enrichment
Grade/Age Levels:	Grades 10–11
Description:	The Architecture Department will offer an intensive 4-week in-residence workshop designed for high school students considering architecture as a career or developing a design portfolio. Students are presented an in-depth view of the career through hands-on experience in studio design exercises, lectures, projects, and field trips. Activities cover architectural design and history, computer applications, building science, structural engineering, and site planning. Studios and lectures are taught by the faculty of the College of Architecture and Environmental Design. Education and career advising are integral elements of the program.

Program:	**Camp Ocean Pines**
Contact:	Chris Cameron, Executive Director
Address:	Camp Ocean Pines 1473 Randall Drive Cambria, CA 93428
Phone:	805-927-0254
Fax:	805-927-2610
E-mail:	admin@campoceanpines.org
Web site:	http://www.campoceanpines.org
Program Type:	Math, Sciences, Engineering, and Computer Science/Technology
Grade/Age Levels:	Ages 8–15
Description:	These weeklong overnight camps provide four to six specialty activities each morning session for students to choose from including marine biology, primitive skills (such as bow and arrow making), and arts and crafts. As part of the program's Ocean Adventures Camp, student visit the Monterey Bay Aquarium.

CALIFORNIA

Program:	**Digital Media Academy**
Contact:	Ms. Rachel Harding, Operations Manager
Address:	Digital Media Academy 1925 Winchester Blvd., Ste. 109 Campbell, CA 95008
Phone:	866-656-3342
Fax:	408-374-4111
E-mail:	info@digitalmediaacademy.org
Web site:	http://www.digitalmediaacademy.org; http://www.digitalmediaadventures.com
Program Type:	Math, Sciences, Engineering, and Computer Science/Technology
Grade/Age Levels:	Ages 9–19
Description:	Digital Media Academy provides summer residential and day computer camps for teens as well as youth (ages 9–13) at locations including Stanford University, University of Texas at Austin, and University of California, San Diego. The Digital Media Academy is a nationally recognized organization offering hands-on learning experiences in a broad range of digital media technologies.

Program:	Economics for Leaders (EFL)
Address:	Economics for Leaders Foundation for Teaching Economics (FTE) 260 Russell Blvd., Ste. B Davis, CA 95616-3839
Phone:	530-757-4630
Fax:	530-757-4636
E-mail:	information@fte.org
Web site:	http://www.fte.org
Program Type:	Leadership/Service/Volunteer
Grade/Age Levels:	Grade 11
Description:	This one-week program on economics and leadership has programs at various sites across the U.S. The Economics for Leaders programs are open to students completing their junior year in high school. These leadership retreats are held on prestigious college campuses throughout the United States and combine leadership and economics instruction. Economics professors and nationally recognized leadership facilitators lead in-depth discussions and activities designed to teach participants to understand and appreciate different leadership styles, develop insight into economic behavior, and foster an economic way of thinking about public policy choices. FTE bases the EFL curriculum on experiential learning, with activities, lessons, and discussions held in both indoor and outdoor settings.

CALIFORNIA

Program:	**Education Program for Gifted Youth (EPGY)**
Contact:	Gina Freeman, Program Coordinator
Address:	Stanford University
	Ventura Hall
	220 Panama Street
	Stanford, CA 94305
Phone:	1-800-372-3749 ext. 325
Fax:	650-614-2383
E-mail:	epgysummer@epgy.stanford.edu
Web site:	http://epgy.stanford.edu/summer/institutes.html
Program Type:	Academic Enrichment
Grade/Age Levels:	Grades 6–11
Description:	The EPGY Summer Institutes are 3-week and 4-week residential programs for academically talented and motivated high school students. The Summer Institutes provide an opportunity for these students to enrich and accelerate their academic pursuits and to meet others who share their interests and abilities.

Summer Institute participants live in supervised Stanford housing and are taught by Stanford instructors. Students engage in intensive study in a single course, and they are introduced to topics not typically presented at the high school level. The instructors are assisted by undergraduate and graduate student mentors who have expertise in the course subject areas. These mentors serve a dual role of Residential Counselor and Teaching Assistant so that the academic and social aspects of the program are tightly integrated. EPGY also offers a middle school program.

Program:	**Idyllwild Arts Summer Program**
Contact:	Ms. Diane Dennis, Registrar
Address:	Idyllwild Arts Box 38, 52500 Temecula Rd. Idyllwild, CA 92549
Phone:	951-659-2171 ext. 2365
Fax:	951-655-4552
E-mail:	summer@idyllwildarts.org
Web site:	http://www.idyllwildarts.org
Program Type:	Fine, Performing, and Visual Arts
Grade/Age Levels:	Ages 5–18
Description:	Since 1950, the Idyllwild Arts Summer Program has offered intensive workshops in dance, film-video, music, theatre, visual arts, and creative writing to students of all ages and abilities, including families.

CALIFORNIA

Program:	**InnerSpark**
Contact:	Mr. Robert Jaffe, Director
Address:	InnerSpark, California State School for the Arts 1010 Hurley Way, Suite 185 Sacramento, CA 95825
Phone:	916-274-5815
Fax:	916-274-5814
E-mail:	rjaffe@innerspark.us
Web site:	http://www.innerspark.us
Program Type:	Fine, Performing, and Visual Arts
Grade/Age Levels:	Grades 9–12
Description:	From July 12 through August 9, 2008, a talented group of high school students will receive intensive training from professionals in music, theatre, video and film, visual arts, dance, creative writing, and animation on the campus of California Institute of the Arts, in Valencia. Camp has a competitive application process with a deadline of February 29, 2008. Financial aid is available for California residents.

Program:	**Internal Drive Tech Camps**
Address:	ID Tech Camps Client Services Representative 42 West Campbell Ave., Ste. 301 Campbell, CA 95008
Phone:	888-709-8324
Fax:	408-871-2228
E-mail:	info@internalDrive.com
Web site:	http://www.internaldrive.com
Program Type:	Math, Sciences, Engineering, and Computer Science/Technology
Grade/Age Levels:	Ages 7–17
Description:	These weeklong day and overnight computer camps are held at 50 universities nationwide including Stanford University and UCLA. At the camps, students learn to create video games, Web sites, digital movies, and more. Students also take part in other activities such as photography, team sports, and language studies.

CALIFORNIA

Program:	**Occidental College Summer Oceanology Program**
Contact:	Dr. Gary Martin, Program Director
Address:	Summer Oceanology Program Occidental College Department of Biology 1600 Campus Rd. Los Angeles, CA 90041-3314
Phone:	323-259-2890
Fax:	323-341-4974
E-mail:	gmartin@oxy.edu
Web site:	http://www.oxy.edu/oxy/marinebio/summer; http://departments.oxy.edu/marinebio/summer
Program Type:	Math, Sciences, Engineering, and Computer Science/Technology
Grade/Age Levels:	Grades 12–20
Description:	This introductory course in marine biology is offered to 24 students who have completed their junior year of high school and it carries college credit for a total of four semesters. Mondays through Thursdays are lectures and labs covering chemical and physical oceanography; the classification and natural history of plankton, algae, invertebrates, fish and marine mammals; marine ecology; techniques for studying organisms and their habitats; and the effects of pollution. Fridays will be spent aboard a research vessel collecting organisms and learning how to investigate selected habitats between the mainland and Catalina Island. Students will live in a college dorm under the supervision of Oxy students who organize a variety of activities including trips to Disneyland, museums, and the beach. Guest scientists will talk about career options and the Oxy Admissions Staff will discuss the college application process. The program provides a strong introduction to marine biology, a taste of college life, and a fun summer in the Los Angeles area.

Program:	Quest Scholars Program
Address:	QuestBridge 120 Hawthorne Ave., Ste. 103 Palo Alto, CA 94301
Phone:	650-331-3280; 888-275-2054
Fax:	650-653-2516
E-mail:	questions@questbridge.org
Web site:	http://www.questbridge.org
Program Type:	Academic Enrichment
Grade/Age Levels:	Grade 11
Description:	The QuestBridge College Prep Scholarship prepares outstanding low-income high school juniors to become successful applicants to leading colleges. Past scholarship awards have included full scholarship for college summer programs, personalized one-on-one college admissions counseling, and invitations to QuestBridge College Preparatory Conferences held on college campuses around the country. Students who apply for the College Prep Scholarship have a head start on the QuestBridge College Match, a program that pairs high-achieving, low-income high school seniors with admission and full 4-year scholarships to QuestBridge partner colleges, including Amherst College, Pomona College, Princeton University, Rice University, Stanford University, Williams College, and Yale University.

CALIFORNIA

Program:	**The Salk Institute for Biological Studies High School Summer Enrichment Program**
Contact:	Dona Mapston, Science Education Specialist
Address:	The Salk Institute for Biological Studies P.O. Box 85800 San Diego, CA 92186-5800
Phone:	858-453-4100
Fax:	858-550-9960
E-mail:	mapston@salk.edu
Web site:	http://www.salk.edu/education/education_summer.php?sid=education
Program Type:	Internships/Paid Positions
Grade/Age Levels:	Ages 16–18
Description:	Students from throughout the San Diego area gather at the Salk Institute every summer to participate in hands-on laboratory experiences under the mentorship of a Salk scientist. Founded more than 30 years ago, the program helps fulfill Dr. Jonas Salk's vision of providing opportunities for local high school students to experience life in a scientific laboratory, and explore the possibility of a career in science. Throughout the 8-week program, which includes one nonpaid training week and a 7-week paid internship, students are involved with a full-time research project as well as enrichment activities. Students learn how to formulate and test hypotheses, prepare experiments, and draw conclusion from data. They also learn to maintain laboratory notebooks and take part in regular lab meetings and group discussions. At the end of the program, students present their research projects to their mentors, lab members, and families. Applicants must be San Diego county residents and be able to commit to 40 hours a week for the duration of the program.

Program:	**Santa Clara University Summer Engineering Seminar (SES)**
Contact:	James Lindfelt, SES Coordinator
Address:	Santa Clara University School of Engineering 500 El Camino Real Santa Clara, CA 95053-4728
Phone:	408-554-4728
E-mail:	summerengineeringseminar@scu.edu
Web site:	http://www.scu.edu/engineering/undergraduate/ses.cfm
Program Type:	Math, Sciences, Engineering, and Computer Science/Technology
Grade/Age Levels:	Grades 9–11
Description:	The SES is a special summer experience for high school students who have an interest in science, mathematics, and engineering. The program is designed to acquaint high school students with the engineering profession, the academic expectations of college, and university life. It provides participants with a chance to explore the possibilities of engineering as a career while living in a university residence hall. Participants take specially designed courses taught by engineering faculty that spans the range of the field of engineering. Courses are a mix of interactive lectures and interactive activities and labs. If accepted, this program has no cost to participants outside of transportation to and from the university. Women and other underrepresented groups in the field of engineering are highly encouraged to apply.

CALIFORNIA

Program:	**Stanford Medical Youth Science Program (SMYSP)**
Contact:	Ms. Judith Ned, Executive Director
Address:	Stanford Medical Youth Science Program Stanford University Stanford Prevention Research Center/Hoover Pavilion 211 Quarry Road, Room N229 Stanford, CA 94305-5705
Phone:	650-498-4514
Fax:	650-725-6247
E-mail:	youth.science@stanford.edu
Web site:	http://smysp.stanford.edu/education/summerPrograms/index.html
Program Type:	Math, Sciences, Engineering, and Computer Science/Technology
Grade/Age Levels:	Grades 9–12
Description:	The Stanford Medical Youth Science Program (SMYSP) offers a 5-week summer residential program held on Stanford's campus for low-income high school students interested in science, medicine, and health. Low-income students from any ethnic background are welcome to apply. SMYSP selects 24 high school students who live and attend schools in Northern and Central California. Ten Stanford University undergraduate students direct the Summer Residential Program and serve as counselors and mentors. The student counselors live with the high school students in a residential house on the Stanford University campus 7 days a week, including weekends. Please note that SMYSP is not a program for gifted students.

Program:	**Summer of Art College Prep Program**
Address:	Summer of Art College Prep Program Otis College of Art and Design 9045 Lincoln Blvd. Los Angeles, CA 90045
Phone:	310-665-6864; 800-527-6847
Fax:	310-665-6854
E-mail:	soa@otis.edu
Web site:	http://www.otis.edu/index.php?id=172
Program Type:	Fine, Performing, and Visual Arts
Grade/Age Levels:	Ages 15 and up
Description:	Otis College of Art and Design Summer of Art is an intensive college prep art and design program for students 15 and older. Serious young artists seeking to strengthen and enhance their art skills, as well as students with limited art training, are invited to participate. Area(s) of concentration include architecture, animation, fashion design, graphic design, illustration, life drawing, digital media, digital photography, product design, painting, and black and white photography. Students can earn college credit for completing the courses.

CALIFORNIA

Program:	**Summer Science Program**
Contact:	Mr. Richard Bowdon, Executive Director
Address:	Summer Science Program 108 Whiteberry Dr. Cary, NC 27519
Phone:	866-728-0999
Fax:	954-862-3051
E-mail:	info@summerscience.org
Web site:	http://www.summerscience.org
Program Type:	Math, Sciences, Engineering, and Computer Science/Technology
Grade/Age Levels:	Rising grades 11 and 12
Description:	One of the longest running and most successful precollege enrichment programs, SSP offers motivated students an exciting immersion into real-world, hands-on science. Working in teams of three, students perform an astronomical research project from start to finish: They determine the orbit of an asteroid from their own observations, measurements, and software. College-level lectures in astronomy, physics, calculus, and programming provide the practical and theoretical tools for each student to understand what he or she is doing and why. Although the pace is challenging, the emphasis is on cooperation, not competition. This 6-week residential program includes behind-the-scenes field trips to places like Jet Propulsion Lab or the Very Large Array. Established at Thacher School in 1959, SSP now takes place at two campuses: New Mexico Tech in Socorro, NM, and Happy Valley School in Ojai, CA (northwest of Los Angeles). The curriculum is identical at the two campuses.

Program:	University of California–Davis Young Scholars Program
Contact:	Dr. Rick Pomeroy, Program Director
Address:	University of California School of Education One Shields Ave. Davis, CA 95616-8579
Phone:	530-752-0622
E-mail:	jrpomeroy@ucdavis.edu
Web site:	http://ysp.ucdavis.edu
Program Type:	Math, Sciences, Engineering, and Computer Science/Technology
Grade/Age Levels:	Grades 10–11
Description:	The UC Davis Young Scholars Program is a summer residential research program designed to expose 40 high achieving high school sophomores and juniors to the world of original research in the natural sciences with emphases on the biological, environmental, and agricultural sciences. Participants in the 2007 UCD-YSP will work one-on-one with research faculty and research groups in state of the art laboratories for 6 weeks.

CALIFORNIA

Program:	**University of California–Irvine COSMOS**
Contact:	Ms. Melina Duarte, Assistant Director
Address:	University of California-Irvine Center for Educational Partnerships University Research Park 5171 California Ave., Ste. 150 Irvine, CA 92697-2505
Phone:	949-824-6806
Fax:	949-824-1371
E-mail:	cosmos@uci.edu
Web site:	http://www.cosmos.uci.edu; http://www.ucop.edu/cosmos
Program Type:	Math, Sciences, Engineering, and Computer Science/Technology
Grade/Age Levels:	Grades 8–12
Description:	The California State Summer School for Mathematics and Science (COSMOS) is a month-long residential academic experience for CA residents who are top high school students in mathematics and science. The COSMOS courses address topics not traditionally taught in high schools: astronomy, computer science, wetlands ecology, ocean science, robotics, neuroscience, cognitive science, game theory, volcanology, and more. Students may apply for need-based financial aid through the application process. Full and partial scholarships are awarded to applicants from California to help with the cost of tuition.

COSMOS is also offered at the following locations:
* University of California, San Diego
  Jacobs School of Engineering
  9500 Gilman Dr., MC 0429
  La Jolla, CA 92093-9429
  858-822-4361
  858-822-3903
  cosmos@soe.ucsd.edu
  http://www.jacobsschool.ucsd.edu/cosmos
* University of California, Santa Cruz
  http://epc.ucsc.edu/cosmos

Program:	**University of Southern California Exploration of Architecture Summer Program**
Contact:	Ms. Jennifer Park
Address:	University of Southern California
School of Architecture
Watt Hall, Ste. 204
Los Angeles, CA 90089-0291
Phone:	213-740-2420; 800-281-8616
Fax:	213-740-8884
E-mail:	jenpark@usc.edu; uscarch@usc.edu
Web site:	http://arch.usc.edu/page_2770.jsp;
http://www.usc.edu/summer
Program Type:	Academic Enrichment
Grade/Age Levels:	Grades 10–12
Description:	The School of Architecture offers 2- or 4-week programs for high school students who have no previous experience but are interested in architecture. The USC Exploration of Architecture program provides high school students from across the country and the world with an intensive and in-depth introduction to the world of architecture and the experience of an architectural education.

CALIFORNIA

Program:	**University of Southern California Summer Seminars for High School Students**
Contact:	Sonny Hayes, Director, Youth Programs
Address:	Summer Seminars for High School Students University of Southern California The Office of Summer and Special Programs 979 W. Jefferson Boulevard Los Angeles, CA 90089-7009
Phone:	213-740-5679
Fax:	213-740-6417
E-mail:	summer@usc.edu
Web site:	http://www.usc.edu/dept/admissions/programs/summmer/seminars.shtml
Program Type:	Academic Enrichment; Math, Sciences, Engineering, and Computer Science/Technology; Fine, Performing, and Visual Arts
Grade/Age Levels:	Grades 6 and up
Description:	Summer Seminars for High School Students allow students to spend 4 weeks living on the USC campus and earn three hours of elective credit. This program is open to high school sophomores, juniors, and seniors. The Summer Seminars meet Monday through Friday in lecture, discussion, laboratory, or field trip mode. The Seminars teach art in the context of performance, and science in the context of contemporary problem solving. *The Summer Science Program for Middle School Boys, Summer Science Program for Middle School Girls*, and *Science Camp for High School Girls* are one-week programs that allow students to learn marine biology and oceanography on Catalina Island. *Exploration of Architecture* allows high school students to discover what architecture and design are all about in a 2- or 4-week program that includes tours and lectures, design studios, and projects.

CALIFORNIA

Program:	**Young Engineering and Science Scholars**
Contact:	Luz Rivas, Program Manager, Young Engineering and Science Scholars
Address:	California Institute of Technology 1200 E. California Blvd. Mail Code 255-86 Pasadena, CA 91125-8600
Phone:	626-395-6208
Fax:	626-395-1736
E-mail:	yess@caltech.edu
Web site:	http://www.yess.caltech.edu
Program Type:	Math, Sciences, Engineering, and Computer Science/Technology
Grade/Age Levels:	Rising 12th only
Description:	For the past decade Caltech has offered this program to promising high school students from economically disadvantaged and underrepresented minority backgrounds. It provides an enrichment program to stimulate their interest in the sciences. The program was successful insofar as the percentage of participants who chose to pursue higher education in the sciences was very high.

CALIFORNIA

COLORADO

Program:	**Crow Canyon Archaeology Camps**
Contact:	Ms. Debra Miller, Registrar
Address:	Ancestral Pueblo Culture of Mesa Verde Region Crow Canyon Archaeological Center 23390 Rd. K Cortez, CO 81321-9908
Phone:	970-565-8975
Fax:	970-565-4859
E-mail:	summercamp@crowcanyon.org; dmiller@crowcanyon.org
Web site:	http://www.crowcanyon.org/archaeology_ adventures/summer_camps.asp
Program Type:	Academic Enrichment
Grade/Age Levels:	Grades 6–12
Description:	Students work with Crow Canyon archaeologists while receiving an introduction to archaeology and Southwestern prehistory. Middle school students take a one-week session; high school students may take either the one-week excavation course or the 3-week field school.

Program:	Frontier Summer Program
Address:	Center for Innovative and Talented Youth University of Denver College of Education 1981 S. University Blvd. Denver, CO 80208
Phone:	303-871-3408
Fax:	303-871-2566
E-mail:	city@du.edu
Web site:	http://www.du.edu/education/ces; http://www.du.edu/city/programs/summer-programs/frontier-program.html
Program Type:	Academic Enrichment
Grade/Age Levels:	Grades 6–8
Description:	Participants attend this transitional 2-week residential experience at the University of Denver and focus on one course of study that may be either an enrichment opportunity or an initial academic acceleration experience. Students qualify for this program with EXPLORE scores as a sixth grader, ACT or SAT scores, or a portfolio. Participants are engaged in a rich residential experience to complement their academic and enrichment work. The Frontier Program serves to help students move from enrichment work to a more intensive study with a dynamic group of high-interest peers.

Program:	**Keystone Mountain Adventures (KMA)**
Contact:	Mr. Joel Egbert, Summer Programs Director
Address:	Keystone Science School Keystone Mountain Adventures 1628 Saints John Rd. Keystone, CO 80435
Phone:	970-468-2098
Fax:	970-468-7769
E-mail:	jegbert@keystone.org
Web site:	http://www.keystone.org/kss/kma.html
Program Type:	Leadership/Service/Volunteer; Math, Sciences, Engineering, and Computer Science/Technology
Grade/Age Levels:	Ages 14–17
Description:	The Keystone Mountain Adventures program uses hands-on experiential education and the exciting adventures of the Colorado wilderness to create an experience that any adventurous 14 to 17-year-old would enjoy. In sessions of 1 to 2 weeks, students will spend time camping in the Colorado Rocky Mountains, rafting in the famous Brown's canyon on the Arkansas river, and rock climbing using top-rope belay systems. Students will enjoy scenic surroundings and educational lessons in forest ecology, aquatic ecology, and geology. Rock climbing is not included in the one-week session. Keystone Science School also offers summer youth programs for all ages. Visit the Web site to request a brochure, or to register for a session. The program also offers the Counselor Assistant Program, designed for teens 14–17 years that have an interest and a desire to develop their leadership skills. Experience the Rockies with future leaders and take home an adventure you will never forget!

Program:	Rocky Mountain Talent Search (RMTS)
Contact:	Dr. Amy Rushneck, Director
Address:	Rocky Mountain Talent Search Center for Innovative and Talented Youth University of Colorado College of Education 1981 S. University Blvd. Denver, CO 80208
Phone:	303-871-3408
Fax:	303-871-2566
E-mail:	city@du.edu
Web site:	http://www.du.edu/city/programs/year-round-programs/rocky-mountain-talent-search.html
Program Type:	Academic Enrichment
Grade/Age Levels:	Grades 3–9
Description:	The University of Denver is one of four institutions in the country operating an academic talent search program based on above-level testing and optimal match. RMTS offers opportunities for academically talented third- through ninth-grade students in New Mexico, Nevada, Utah, Colorado, Wyoming, Idaho, and Montana. RMTS participants take the SAT, ACT, or EXPLORE examinations to evaluate their strengths, to gain experience, and to qualify for awards and special programming. All participants receive a certificate of recognition, score interpretation information, and a regional summer opportunities guide. High-scoring students are invited to a regional RMTS Awards Ceremony.

Program:	University of Northern Colorado Summer Enrichment Program
Contact:	Ms. Tess Henkelman, Administrative Assistant
Address:	Summer Enrichment Program University of Northern Colorado Campus Box 141 Greeley, CO 80639
Phone:	970-351-2683
Fax:	970-351-1061
E-mail:	sep@unco.edu
Web site:	http://www.unco.edu/sep
Program Type:	Academic Enrichment
Grade/Age Levels:	Grades 5–10
Description:	This is a residential academic program in which students enroll in four 75-minute classes for 10 days of instruction. The courses are created to address the abilities, needs, and interests of bright students, and curriculum is developed and differentiated according to the basic principles of gifted education. In addition to taking classes, students are exposed to a variety of activities that allow for interaction and socialization with other gifted students. Daytime courses will include art, computers and technology, creative writing, cultures, debate, drama, dance, history, mathematics, music/band/orchestra/choir, and science.

Program:	**Center for Creative Youth at Wesleyan University**
Contact:	Dr. Herbert Sheppard, General Director
Address:	Center for Creative Youth at Wesleyan University Capitol Region Education Council Center for Creative Youth 15 Vernon St. Hartford, CT 06106
Phone:	860-757-6391; 860-685-3307
E-mail:	ccy@crec.org; hsheppard@crec.org
Web site:	http://www.crec.org/ccy
Program Type:	Fine, Performing, and Visual Arts; Leadership/Service/Volunteer
Grade/Age Levels:	Grades 10–12
Description:	This 5-week residential program for precollege students emphasizes the following creative areas: creative writing, dance, filmmaking, music, musical theater, photography, technical theater, theater, and visual arts.

CONNECTICUT

CONNECTICUT

Program:	**Project Oceanology**
Address:	Project Oceanology University of Connecticut Avery Point Campus 1084 Shennecossett Rd. Groton, CT 06340
Phone:	860-445-9007; 800-364-8472
Fax:	860-449-8008
E-mail:	oceanology@aol.com
Web site:	http://www.oceanology.org/kidsprogram.html
Program Type:	Math, Sciences, Engineering, and Computer Science/Technology
Grade/Age Levels:	Grades 5–12
Description:	Project Oceanology offers the following programs:

- *Ocean Camp*: Students entering grades 6–7 take part in a coastal habitat study, students entering grades 8–9 take part in a nearshore habitat study, and students who have entering grades 10–12 take part in an offshore habitat study.
- *Ocean Explorer Academy*: This program is a one-week commuter program for students who have completed sixth grade.
- *Ocean Diversity Institute*: This offers camp programs for students in ninth grade.
- *Summer Marine Studies*: In this 3-week program, students conduct in-depth research projects on oceanology.

Program:	**Summer Institute for the Gifted (SIG)**
Address:	Summer Institute for the Gifted River Plaza 9 W. Broad St. Stamford, CT 06902-3788
Phone:	203-399-5455; 866-303-4744
E-mail:	sig.info@giftedstudy.com
Web site:	http://www.giftedstudy.com
Program Type:	Academic Enrichment
Grade/Age Levels:	Grades K–11
Description:	This program is an opportunity for students to take part in numerous academic activities and classes introducing them to college level work, as well as social growth opportunities and cultural awareness. To qualify for admission, students must have been chosen through a talent search program, scored above the 95th percentile in a nationally normed standardized exam, be part of a gifted program, or have strong recommendations from teachers and school administrators. SIG offers residential programs for students in grades 4–11 at the following sites: Amherst College, Bryn Mawr College, Drew University, Emory University, Princeton University (grades 7–11 only), University of California-Berkeley, University of California Los Angeles, University of Michigan-Ann Arbor, and Vassar College. In addition, day programs for students in grades K–6 are offered at Bryn Mawr College, Fairfield University, Manhattanville College, and Moorestown Friends School. Students can take courses and activities in the following content areas: art, astronomy, biology, business/entrepreneurship, chemistry, computer science, creative writing, current events, engineering, history, law, math, music, performing arts, physics, psychology, science, speech/debate, study skills, and technology.

CONNECTICUT

Program:	**University of Delaware Summer College**
Contact:	Mr. Chuck Shermeyer, Program Coordinator
Address:	Summer College University of Delaware 207 Elliott Hall 26 E. Main St. Newark, DE 19716-1256
Phone:	302-831-6560
Fax:	302-831-4339
E-mail:	summercollege@udel.edu
Web site:	http://summercollege.honors.udel.edu/index.html
Program Type:	Academic Enrichment
Grade/Age Levels:	Grades 10–11
Description:	This program offers a 5-week residential precollege experience for academically talented high school sophomores and juniors. Students stay in an air-conditioned residence hall while earning six to seven college credits. Students will attend a series of academic skill programs, as well as complete two or three courses taught by university faculty. Summer college students can choose to take core courses and/or second summer session courses. A list of courses is available online. Weekend trips and educational, recreational, and social programs are included as part of the program. Students also may apply for partial merit- and need-based financial aid to help cover the costs of the program.

DELAWARE

Program:	**Catholic University of America Precollege Programs**
Contact:	Ms. Harriet Nokuri, Director of Summer Sessions
Address:	Precollege Programs Catholic University of America CUA Office of Summer Sessions 330 Pangborn Hall 620 Michigan Ave. NE Washington, DC 20064
Phone:	202-319-5257
Fax:	202-319-6725
E-mail:	cua-summers@cua.edu; nokuri@cua.edu
Web site:	http://summer.cua.edu/precollege
Program Type:	Academic Enrichment
Grade/Age Levels:	Grades 4–12
Description:	The *CUA Summer College* program for rising high school juniors and seniors, allows students to become immersed in college life and earn credits to be applied to their college education. The *Experiences in Architecture* program, for rising high school juniors and seniors, is an intensive 3-week architecture workshop, in which students tour design firms and construction sites and create models and drawings. The *Lion Drummers Percussion Workshop* allows students in grades 4–12 to work with a master instructor while exploring rhythm, groove, and the "language" of music. The *Opera Institute for Young Singers* provides a 3-week pre-professional performance training program in Italian art songs for serious vocal students ages 15–18. The *KEYs to Empowering Youth* program is for young women ages 11–13.

DISTRICT OF COLUMBIA

Program:	**Discover the World of Communication**
Contact:	Sarah Menke-Fish, Assistant Professor and Director, Discover the World of Communication
Address:	American University School of Communication 4400 Massachusetts Ave. NW, MGC 300 Washington, DC 20016
Phone:	205-885-2098; 202-885-2061
Fax:	202-885-2019 (fax)
E-mail:	smenke@american.edu
Web site:	http://www.soc.american.edu/highschool.html
Program Type:	Fine, Performing, and Visual Arts
Grade/Age Levels:	Grades 9–12
Description:	Do you have a broadcast bug or a knack for film and writing? Then, the American University School of Communication has a summer program ready to teach you broadcasting, news- and sports-writing, filmmaking, digital editing, and anything else you need to satisfy your communications cravings. The 4-week residential program includes more than 30 noncredit, certificate courses, such as scriptwriting and video production.

Program:	Science and Engineering Apprenticeship Program (SEAP)
Contact:	M. Phillips, Director
Address:	Science and Engineering Apprenticeship Program The George Washington University Department of Defense 1776 G St. NW, Ste. 171 Washington, DC 20052
Phone:	202-994-2234
E-mail:	seap@gwu.edu
Web site:	http://www.gwseap.net/default.asp; http://www.asee.org/seap/index.cfm
Program Type:	Internships/Paid Positions
Grade/Age Levels:	Rising grades 10 and up
Description:	This program offers various scientific, engineering, and math research studies at various locations. Students are encouraged to apply on site. The SEAP office places academically talented students, ranging from middle school through college in Department of Defense (DOD) laboratories for 8 continuous weeks during the summer. These students, who usually possess a diverse background and have interest in sciences and mathematics, work closely with scientists and engineers who act as their mentors. The program offers students a unique and positive experience in their fields of interest, thus encouraging them to pursue careers in science and engineering.

DISTRICT OF COLUMBIA

Program:	**Acadia Institute of Oceanography (AIO)**
Contact:	Sheryl Gilmore, Executive Director
Address:	Acadia Institute of Oceanography P.O. Box 2220 St. Augustine, FL 32085-2220
Phone:	800-375-0058
Fax:	904-461-3331
E-mail:	info@acadiainstitute.com
Web site:	http://www.acadiainstitute.com
Program Type:	Academic Enrichment
Grade/Age Levels:	Ages 12–18
Description:	AIO is a summer camp program for marine science studies based in Seal Harbor, ME. Our unique program is designed for motivated young people between the ages of 12 and 18 who want to learn and have fun in the pristine ocean environment next to Acadia National Park. Sessions are coeducational. AIO offers basic and advanced sessions taught by our professional staff.

Summer Address (June 1 to Aug. 31):
Acadia Institute of Oceanography
P.O. Box 285
Seal Harbor, ME 04685
Phone: 207-276-9825

Program:	Seacamp Association
Contact:	James Stoll
Address:	Seacamp Association, Inc. 1300 Big Pine Ave. Big Pine Key, FL 33043
Phone:	305-872-2331; 877-SEACAMP
Fax:	305-872-2555
E-mail:	info@seacamp.org
Web site:	http://www.seacamp.org
Program Type:	Math, Sciences, Engineering, and Computer Science/Technology
Grade/Age Levels:	Ages 12–17
Description:	Seacamp Association is a nonprofit, marine science education facility located on Big Pine Key in the tropical Florida Keys adjacent to Looe Key and Florida's fragile coral reefs. During the summer, Seacamp offers three 18-day camp sessions for teens 12–17, focusing on marine science and scuba diving. Seacamp also offers unique program trips to the grass and sponge flats of the only remaining coral reef in America. During the school year, Newfound Harbor Marine Institute at Seacamp offers programming for schools from 3–30 days for students in fourth grade through college.

FLORIDA

Program:	**University of Miami Summer Scholar Programs**
Address:	University of Miami Summer Scholar Programs P.O. Box 248005 Coral Gables, FL 33124-1610
Phone:	800-788-3986
Fax:	305-284-2620
Web site:	http://www.miami.edu/summerscholars
Program Type:	Academic Enrichment
Grade/Age Levels:	Grades 11–12
Description:	The Summer Scholar Programs are designed for high school students currently in their sophomore or junior year. They must have a 3.0 grade point average to apply. Students can study one of nine programs: broadcast journalism, engineering, filmmaking, forensic investigation, global politics, health and medicine, marine science, sports management, and studio and communication arts. At the completion of the program, participants will earn between four and six college credit hours. Attendees can expect to live on campus, have plenty of hands-on learning in the classroom, and go on off-campus excursions to area attractions such as South Beach and Florida Marlins baseball games. The main goal of the program is to give high school students a realistic introduction to college life.

Program:	**Firespark! School for Gifted Students in Fine Arts and Communication**
Contact:	Ms. Alyssa Maddox, Co-Director
Address:	Firespark! School for Gifted Students in Fine Arts and Communication Brenau University 500 Washington St. SE Gainesville, GA 30501
Phone:	770-534-6741; 800-252-5119 ext. 6741
E-mail:	firespark@brenau.edu
Web site:	http://www.firespark.org
Program Type:	Fine, Performing, and Visual Arts
Grade/Age Levels:	Ages 13–18
Description:	Firespark! is a coeducational program for students gifted in theatre, dance, music, art, communication and business. *Firespark! Fine Arts and Communication* features classes taught by practicing professionals and university faculty in the areas of art and design, dance, drama, communication, and music. Classes in a variety of science areas, premedicine, physical and occupational therapy, and nursing will be offered in the *Firespark! Medical Scholars* program. The *Firespark! Legal Scholars* students will develop their legal skills through the preparation and presentation of a case for a mock trial.

GEORGIA

Program:	**Habitat for Humanity**
Address:	Habitat AmeriCorps/VISTA Partner Service Center Habitat for Humanity International 121 Habitat St. Americus, GA 31709-3498
Phone:	229-924-6935 ext. 2551 or 2552
E-mail:	publicinfo@habitat.org
Web site:	http://www.habitat.org
Program Type:	Leadership/Service/Volunteer
Grade/Age Levels:	All ages
Description:	Students can earn stipends and educational awards by serving communities through these Corporation for National Service partnerships. Habitat for Humanity, in partnership with the Corporation for National and Community Service, provides hundreds of service opportunities for people of diverse ages and backgrounds. CNCS, an integral part of USA Freedom Corps, supports dynamic volunteer service programs such as AmeriCorps State/National, AmeriCorps VISTA, AmeriCorps NCCC, and Senior Corps.

GEORGIA

Program:	**Savannah College of Art and Design (SCAD) Summer Seminars**
Address:	Summer Seminars Savannah College of Art and Design Admission Department P.O. Box 2072 Savannah, GA 31402-2072
Phone:	800-869-7223
E-mail:	info@scad.edu; admission@scad.edu
Web site:	http://www.scad.edu/admission/summer_programs/index.cfm
Program Type:	Fine, Performing, and Visual Arts
Grade/Age Levels:	Grades 10–12
Description:	SCAD Summer Seminars are residential or nonresidential summer workshops in Savannah and Atlanta designed for high school students who have completed their freshman, sophomore or junior years. Topics include animation, digital photography, drawing, fashion, painting, and sequential art. Students are housed in a college residence hall, where they receive meals on the college meal plan.

GEORGIA

Program:	**Spelman College Summer Programs**
Contact:	Ms. L. M. Jamila Canady, Interim Director
Address:	Continuing Education Spelman College 350 Spelman Lane, SW Campus Box 849 Atlanta, GA 30314-4399
Phone:	404-270-5365; 404-270-5367
Fax:	404-270-53689
E-mail:	sakiele@spelman.edu
Web site:	http://www.spelman.edu/academics/continuing/summerprograms.shtml
Program Type:	Academic Enrichment
Grade/Age Levels:	Grades 6–12
Description:	The *College Prep Institute* is a 2-week residential, college preparatory program for young women who are rising sophomores and juniors in high school. The Institute features hands-on Internet sessions, featuring lessons on test preparation, leadership, and college preparation. Contact Sharon Akiele at 404-270-5369 for more information. The *Children's Dance and Drama Program* offers three components: the regular term (September through May), the 6-week Summer Dance and Drama Institute, and the Children's Performance Theatre. Contact Marvette Baldwin at 404-270-5721 or mbaldwin@spelman.edu for more information. Spelman College also offers the following programs:

- *Atlanta Public Schools Science and Mathematics Summer Enrichment Academy*;
- *Early College Program* (a residential college preparatory program);
- *HHMI Summer Science Program*; and
- *Morehouse/Spelman HCOP PreFreshman Summer Science Program.*

Program:	**Hawaii Preparatory Academy Summer Session**
Contact:	Dr. Olaf Jorgenson, Headmaster
Address:	Hawaii Preparatory Academy Summer Session 65-1692 Kohala Mountain Road Kamuela, HI 96743-8476
Phone:	808-881-4088
Fax:	808-881-4071
E-mail:	summer@hpa.edu
Web site:	http://www.hpa.edu/summer/index.html
Program Type:	Academic Enrichment
Grade/Age Levels:	Grades 6–12
Description:	The Summer Session at Hawaii Preparatory Academy offers academic enrichment and unique study opportunities for 120 boarding and day co-ed students from around the world. Students attend diverse courses such as photography, algebra, dance, golf, Spanish, marine science, SAT prep, and global warming. Weekend excursions to cultural and scientific sites such as Volcanoes National Park, and activities such as kayaking, snorkeling, camping, and hiking are also included. The afternoon athletics program offers students an opportunity to participate in a nationally recognized equestrian program or work toward SCUBA certification.

HAWAII

IDAHO

Program:	**Junior Engineering, Math and Science (JEMS) Summer Workshop**
Address:	University of Idaho College of Engineering Janssen Engineering 125 P.O. Box 441011 Moscow, ID 83844-1011
Phone:	208-855-4934
Fax:	208-885-1399
E-mail:	jems@uidaho.edu
Web site:	http://www.uidaho.edu/engr/jems
Program Type:	Math, Sciences, Engineering, and Computer Science/Technology
Grade/Age Levels:	Grades 12–13
Description:	The University of Idaho College of Engineering sponsors the annual Idaho Junior Engineering, Mathematics, and Science (JEMS) Summer Workshop for students who have completed their junior or senior year of high school. The focus of the workshop is to expose students to engineering problems within technical and social contexts, and to encourage them to enroll in college. This year, JEMS will include lectures and hands-on activities in leadership, engineering design, modeling, and possibly AutoCAD. Students will participate in lab exercises, field trips, computer exercises, and recreational activities. Scholarships are available. The program is July 13–25, 2008; Deadline to apply is May 23.

Program:	**Aerospace Institute Summer Camp**
Contact:	Ms. Diane Jeffers, Associate Director
Address:	Aerospace Institute Summer Camp University of Illinois at Urbana-Champaign 306 Talbot Laboratory 104 S. Wright St. Urbana, IL 61801-2302
Phone:	217-244-8048
Fax:	217-244-0720
E-mail:	dejeffer@uiuc.edu
Web site:	http://www.ae.uiuc.edu/IAI
Program Type:	Math, Sciences, Engineering, and Computer Science/Technology
Grade/Age Levels:	Rising grades 9–12
Description:	This one-week program for high school students offers classroom and hands-on experience in the areas of propulsion systems, theory of flight, aerodynamics, principles of aircraft, and spacecraft design. See Web site for additional programs.

ILLINOIS

Program:	**Ancient Worlds**
Contact:	Mary Pirkl, Director of Education
Address:	Center for American Archeology (CAA)
	P.O. Box 366
	Kampsville, IL 62053
Phone:	618-653-4316
Fax:	618-653-4232
E-mail:	caa@caa-archeology.org
Web site:	http://www.caa-archeology.org
Program Type:	Academic Enrichment
Grade/Age Levels:	Ages 13–17
Description:	In CAA's youth field school, Ancient Worlds, students learn the basics of archeological field excavation, conduct lab work, and explore ancient technologies and skills. Real archeology—really fun! Additional programs are listed on CAA Web site.

Program:	**CAMPWS WaterTEC: Exploring Water Purification**
Contact:	Ms. Sue Herricks, WaterTEC
Address:	CAMPWS WaterTEC: Exploring Water Purification University of Illinois at Urbana-Champaign 201 N. Goodwin Ave. Urbana, IL 61801-2302
Phone:	217-244-9352
E-mail:	sherrcks@uiuc.edu
Web site:	http://www.engr.uiuc.edu/outreach/Ingenious/index.php?id=getinvolved&sub=camps
Program Type:	Math, Sciences, Engineering, and Computer Science/Technology
Grade/Age Levels:	Rising grades 9–12
Description:	Campers will be immersed in the engineering, science, and technology of water purification. Participants will learn about all aspects, from river systems to nanotechnology. Field testing, laboratories, projects, team building, and a week long Water Works competition will help campers develop an understanding of the research behind the new water purification technologies. Sponsored by the Center of Advanced Materials for Purification of Water with Systems (CAMPWS).

ILLINOIS

Program:	The Center for Gifted at National-Louis University Summer Programs
Contact:	Ms. Joan Smutny, Director
Address:	The Center for Gifted at National-Louis University P.O. Box 364 Wilmette, IL 60091
Phone:	847-901-0173
Fax:	847-901-0179
E-mail:	jsmutny@nl.edu
Web site:	http://www.centerforgifted.org
Program Type:	Academic Enrichment
Grade/Age Levels:	Grades K–10
Description:	The Center for Gifted at National-Louis University offers many opportunities for gifted children to explore diverse subjects in a challenging, creative environment, free from pressures of tests and grades, where each child's unique talents and gifts are sensitively nurtured. Current programs offered include *Project 2008*, *Summer Wonders*, and *Worlds of Wisdom and Wonder*. Creativity and critical thinking are inherent in all classes and activities and compromise the framework for teaching. Courses are available for children in kindergarten through grade 10 at many Chicago area locations and at two National-Louis University campuses.

ILLINOIS

Program:	Center for Talent Development (CTD) Summer Program
Address:	Summer Programs Center for Talent Development Northwestern University 617 Dartmouth Pl. Evanston, IL 60208
Phone:	847-491-3782
Fax:	847-467-4283
E-mail:	ctd@northwestern.edu
Web site:	http://www.ctd.northwestern.edu
Program Type:	Academic Enrichment; Math, Sciences, Engineering, and Computer Science/Technology; Leadership/Service/Volunteer
Grade/Age Levels:	Grades PreK–12
Description:	Do you want to complete AP Calculus in just 3 weeks? Are you eager to combine rigorous and engaging academic work with community service and hands-on field experiences designed to help young people develop the knowledge, experience, and leadership skills they need to make a positive impact on society? Students completing grades 4–12 may sign up for one or two 3-week sessions during which they can take one course. More than 100 enrichment, honors, and Advanced Placement courses in the sciences, math, literature, humanities, writing, history, and language—from Engineering and Physics to Youth and Society Honors—are included. Students may reside on Northwestern University's Evanston campus. Classes are held daily from 8:30 a.m. to 2:45 p.m. Weekends are spent exploring Chicago's cultural offerings. Civic Leadership Institute participants live in Chicago. CTD also offers a joint program with Case Western Reserve University. This program offers honor classes for students in grades 7–12 on Case Western Reserve's Cleveland campus.

ILLINOIS

Program:	Exploring Your Options and Discover Engineering
Contact:	Mary Weaver, Director
Address:	Exploring Your Options and Discover Engineering University of Illinois at Urbana-Champaign 210 N. Goodwin Ave. Urbana, IL 61801-2302
Phone:	217-333-2860
Fax:	217-244-2488
E-mail:	wyse@uiuc.edu
Web site:	http://www.engr.uiuc.edu/WYSE/EYO/index.html
Program Type:	Math, Sciences, Engineering, and Computer Science/Technology
Grade/Age Levels:	Rising grades 10–12
Description:	*Exploring Your Options* (EYO) is a one-week residential camp that provides students who are interested in math and science a chance to visit and participate in hands-on activities in each of the departments in the College of Engineering. Two sessions are offered and the camps are limited to 40 students each. Exploring Your Options is for students who will be in the 11th or 12th grade in the fall of the current calendar year. *Discover Engineering* is a one–week residential camp for rising sophomores who are interested in math and science. Students will work on several projects that will incorporate different aspects of engineering. The camp is limited to 30 students. Discover Engineering is for students who will be in the 10th grade in the fall of the current year calendar year.

ILLINOIS

Program:	Girls' Adventures in Math, Engineering, and Science Camp (GAMES)
Contact:	Ms. Minosca Alcantara
Address:	G.A.M.E.S. Summer Camp Women in Engineering Program University of Illinois at Urbana-Champaign 206 Engineering Hall, MC-272 1308 W. Green St. Urbana, IL 61801
Phone:	217-244-7673
Fax:	217-244-4794
E-mail:	malcanta@uiuc.edu
Web site:	http://www.engr.uiuc.edu/wie/games/index.php
Program Type:	Math, Sciences, Engineering, and Computer Science/Technology
Grade/Age Levels:	Rising grades 6–9
Description:	This one-week residential program provides academically talented middle school girls the opportunity to explore math, engineering, and science through demonstrations, classroom presentations, hands-on activities, and contact with other women in technical fields. Three camps are offered for different age levels: *Structures Camp* (girls who will be in sixth and seventh grade in the fall); *Computer Science Camp* (girls who will be in seventh and eighth grade in the fall); and *Bioengineering/Chemical Engineering Camp* (girls who will be in the eighth and ninth grade in the fall).

ILLINOIS

Program:	**IMSA Kids Institute**
Address:	IMSA Kids Institute Illinois Mathematics and Science Academy 1500 W. Sullivan Rd. Aurora, IL 60506-1067
Phone:	630-907-5950
Fax:	630-907-5880
E-mail:	summerprograms@imsa.edu
Web site:	http://www.imsa.edu/programs/summer_IMSA/ summer_at_IMSA.php
Program Type:	Math, Sciences, Engineering, and Computer Science/Technology
Grade/Age Levels:	Grades 5–9
Description:	The IMSA Kids Institute offers both day and residential programs. In 2007, the day program offerings included Science Explorers, Computer Explorers, CSI: IMSA E2K+ Style (forensic science techniques), Jazz Explorers, and Summer Sleuths. The 2007 residential programs included Science@IMSA Residential Camps for Boys and Girls (grades 8–9), Math@IMSA (grades 8–9), and Biotech@IMSA (grade 9). Each program lasts approximately one week. Visit the Web site for an updated listing of 2008 programs.

Program:	**National Student Leadership Conference (NSLC)**
Contact:	Dr. Paul Lisnek, Executive Director, Director of Academics
Address:	National Student Leadership Conference Office of Admissions 1 N. Dearborn, 6th Floor Chicago, IL 60602
Phone:	312-873-6974; 800-994-6752
Fax:	312-873-6940
E-mail:	info@nslcleaders.org
Web site:	http://www.nslcleaders.org
Program Type:	Academic Enrichment
Grade/Age Levels:	Grades 9–12
Description:	The National Student Leadership Conference offers high-achieving students the opportunity to explore a future career hands-on while developing essential leadership skills, experiencing life on a college campus, and interacting with a diverse group of students from across the U.S. and around the world. During college-level lectures and interactive career simulations, students will gain insight into one of the following fields: arts, business, engineering, forensic science, government and politics, intelligence and national security, international business, international diplomacy, journalism and mass communication, or law. Domestic programs operate at the University of California-Berkeley, the University of Maryland, American University, and Fordham University. NSLC conducts European programs in Geneva, Switzerland.

ILLINOIS

Program:	**The School of the Art Institute of Chicago Summer Programs**
Address:	The School of the Art Institute of Chicago 37 S. Wabash Ave. Chicago, IL 60603
Phone:	312-899-7458
Fax:	312-899-7448
E-mail:	ecp@saic.edu
Web site:	http://www.saic.edu/ecp
Program Type:	Fine, Performing, and Visual Arts
Grade/Age Levels:	Grades 9–12
Description:	The School of the Art Institute of Chicago offers the following programs:

- *Summer Institute Residency Program*: One of the largest visual-arts-school-based high school programs in the country, the Summer Institute draws students from around the country and abroad. Open only to current high school sophomores, juniors, and seniors for college credit.
- The *Early College Program* offers two sessions during the Summer Institute Residency program in addition to other summer courses without residency requirements. Current high school sophomores, juniors, and seniors may enroll for college credit.
- The *Creative Writing Program*, grades 9–12, is designed for students of all levels and interests, not just beginning writers.

Program:	University of Chicago Summer Program for High School Students
Address:	The University of Chicago The Graham School of General Studies 1427 E. 60th St. Chicago, IL 60637
Phone:	773-834-3792
E-mail:	slopez@uchicago.edu
Web site:	https://summer.uchicago.edu
Program Type:	Math, Sciences, Engineering, and Computer Science/Technology; Fine, Performing, and Visual Arts; Gap Year/Study Abroad/International Travel
Grade/Age Levels:	Grades 9–12
Description:	The University of Chicago offered the following summer programs in 2007 (note that these may be different in 2008):

- *Insight:* In these 3-week courses, students are able to join experts in various fields to have an experiential learning opportunity.
- *Research in the Biological Sciences:* Experience "life at the bench" and learn cutting-edge molecular, cellular, and microbiological research techniques.
- *Stones and Bones:* Join the Field Museum of Natural History's Lance Grande on an expedition digging for fossils.
- *Summer Quarter for High School Students:* Take intensive language study or other courses from the regular college curriculum, and study alongside undergraduates from the University of Chicago and elsewhere.
- *Traveling Academy:* Travel to Greece to study the role of drama and performance in ancient Greek culture.

ILLINOIS

Program:	**Ball State University College of Architecture and Planning (CAP) Summer Workshop**
Contact:	Mr. Brian Hollars, Summer Workshop Coordinator
Address:	Ball State University College of Architecture and Planning 2000 W. University Ave. Muncie, IN 47306
Phone:	765-285-5862
E-mail:	cap@bsu.edu
Web site:	http://www.bsu.edu/cap/workshop
Program Type:	Fine, Performing, and Visual Arts
Grade/Age Levels:	Grades 11–12
Description:	Each spring the College of Architecture and Planning invites outstanding high school juniors and seniors to apply for admission to the CAP Summer Workshop. This workshop is an intensive immersion into the realm of environmental design and problem solving. CAP faculty members bring this program to the participants via a series of exercises that increasingly challenge the young mind and its understanding of the built environment. The exercises are designed to encourage exploration and growth of creativity and uniqueness found in each individual personality.

Program:	**Ball State University High School Summer Journalism Workshops**
Contact:	Mr. Brian Hayes, SES Director
Address:	Ball State University Department of Journalism Secondary Education Services 2000 W. University Ave. Muncie, IN 47306
Phone:	765-289-1241; 800-382-8540
Fax:	765-285-8900
E-mail:	bsuworkshops@bsu.edu; bhayes@bsu.edu
Web site:	http://www.bsujournalismworkshops.com/
Program Type:	Fine, Performing, and Visual Arts
Grade/Age Levels:	Rising grade 12 and up
Description:	More than 400 high school journalists and 50 advisers are expected to come to campus in late July for Ball State's annual summer high school journalism workshops. The Department of Journalism's Secondary Education Services office, which also runs Junior High Journalism Day each fall and High School Journalism Day each spring, is planning the summer events. The week-long summer workshops allow students to study specific areas of journalism with award-winning journalists and publication advisers. The workshop also offers individual school newspaper or yearbook staff camps that allow the entire staff to plan for the year's publications with the help of award-winning instructors.

INDIANA

Program:	Exciting Discoveries for Girls in Engineering (EDGE) Summer Camp
Contact:	Dr. Suzanne Zurn-Birkhimer, Assistant Director
Address:	EDGE Summer Camp Purdue University Women In Engineering Program Civil Engineering Building Room G167 550 Stadium Mall Dr. West Lafayette, IN 47907-2051
Phone:	765-494-3889
Fax:	765-496-1349
E-mail:	zurnbirk@purdue.edu; puwie@ecn.purdue.edu
Web site:	https://engineering.purdue.edu/WIEP/EDGE/index.htm
Program Type:	Math, Sciences, Engineering, and Computer Science/Technology
Grade/Age Levels:	Grades 10–11
Description:	This camp is focused on girls entering their sophomore and junior years in high school, and is designed to better acquaint the participants with opportunities in engineering and how their interests and talents can be utilized in this exciting career. The campers will build their own electronics device, program an experiment using Lego Investigator, and tour engineering laboratories and a production facility.

Program:	**Gifted Education Resource Institute (GERI) Summer Camps**
Contact:	Dr. Rebecca Mann, Gifted Education Resource Institute
Address:	100 N. University St. Beering Hall, Room 5108A West Lafayette, IN 47907-1446
Phone:	765-494-7243
Fax:	765-496-2706
E-mail:	geri@purdue.edu
Web site:	http://www.geri.education.purdue.edu/main/default.html
Program Type:	Academic Enrichment; Math, Sciences, Engineering, and Computer Science/Technology; Fine, Performing, and Visual Arts
Grade/Age Levels:	Grades Pre-K–12
Description:	GERI Summer Camps offer gifted students challenging and enjoyable academic experiences in science, technology, mathematics, the humanities, and the arts, combined with a wide variety of cultural, athletic, and recreational options. Residential students (grades 5–12 only) stay in air-conditioned residence halls and have access to all the resources of Purdue University, a leading Big 10 research university.

INDIANA

Program:	**Introduction to Engineering**
Contact:	Ramzi Bualuan, IEP Director
Address:	Introduction to Engineering University of Notre Dame 384 Fitzpatrick Hall of Engineering Notre Dame, IN 46556-5637
Phone:	574-631-8320
Fax:	574-631-9260
E-mail:	cse@cse.nd.edu; iep@nd.edu
Web site:	http://www.nd.edu/~iep
Program Type:	Math, Sciences, Engineering, and Computer Science/Technology
Grade/Age Levels:	Rising grade 12
Description:	Introduction to Engineering is a 3-week summer program for high school students. Students are given a taste of college life while discovering career opportunities in engineering and receiving an overview of the elements of engineering design and computer programming. Cost includes regular field trips, incidentals, meal plans, and housing.

Program:	**Love Engineering at Purdue (LEAP) Summer Camp**
Contact:	Dr. Suzanne Zurn-Birkhimer, Assistant Director
Address:	LEAP Summer Camp Purdue University Women In Engineering Program Civil Engineering Building, Room G167 550 Stadium Mall Dr., West Lafayette, IN 47907-2051
Phone:	765-494-3889
Fax:	765-496-1349
E-mail:	zurnbirk@purdue.edu; puwie@ecn.purdue.edu
Web site:	https://engineering.purdue.edu/WIEP/LEAP
Program Type:	Math, Sciences, Engineering, and Computer Science/Technology
Grade/Age Levels:	Grades 7–9
Description:	This camp is focused on girls entering grades 7–9. The campers are able to view many engineering laboratories on campus, reassemble a computer, design a Web page, and design and program a robot.

INDIANA

Program:	Operation Catapult
Contact:	Ms. Lisa Norton, Associate Director of Admissions
Address:	Operation Catapult Rose-Hulman Institute of Technology 5500 Wabash Ave. Terre Haute, IN 47803
Phone:	800-248-7448
Fax:	812-877-8941
E-mail:	lisa.norton@rose-hulman.edu
Web site:	http://www.rose-hulman.edu/catapult
Program Type:	Math, Sciences, Engineering, and Computer Science/Technology
Grade/Age Levels:	Grade 11 only
Description:	This 2 ½-week residential program provides campers with an opportunity to investigate some physical phenomena. At Operation Catapult, you'll have a once-in-a-lifetime experience tackling real scientific problems.

Program:	**OPTIONS**
Contact:	Dr. Phil Gerhart, Director, OPTIONS
Address:	University of Evansville College of Engineering and Computer Science 1800 Lincoln Ave. Evansville, IN 47722
Phone:	812-488-2651
Fax:	812-488-2780
E-mail:	tn2@evansville.edu
Web site:	http://options.evansville.edu
Program Type:	Math, Sciences, Engineering, and Computer Science/Technology; Gap Year/Study Abroad/International Travel
Grade/Age Levels:	Grades 10–12
Description:	*OPTIONS for High School Girls* is an all-inclusive residential camp for high-school-aged girls who have passed geometry (or an equivalent math course) and will be in grades 10–12 in the fall of 2008 or the equivalent home school level. Scholarships are available. Students take challenging courses with university professors and job shadow professional female engineers and computer scientists as part of this program. New for 2008 is an optional week of travel to England for an additional fee. Participants can choose to attend just the first week of the program or both weeks. The travel abroad opportunity is not guaranteed to be offered each year. *OPTIONS for Middle School Girls* is a 5-day, 4-night residential camp for middle-school-aged girls who will be in grades 7–9 in the fall. The purpose of this camp is to expose girls to the vast career options made possible with a degree in engineering or computer science.

INDIANA

IOWA

Program:	**Engineering & Beyond Workshop**
Contact:	Ms. Sadie Kohlhaas, Recruitment Coordinator
Address:	Engineering & Beyond Workshop Iowa State University College of Engineering Outreach and Recruitment Office 112 Marston Hall Ames, IA 50011-2011
Phone:	515-294-8355
E-mail:	slk@iastate.edu
Web site:	http://www.eng.iastate.edu/eb
Program Type:	Math, Sciences, Engineering, and Computer Science/Technology
Grade/Age Levels:	Rising grade 12
Description:	The Engineering and Beyond Workshop is a workshop that exposes you to all areas of engineering—it's more than what you think! The workshop is both educational and fun. You will learn about Iowa State's engineering majors, and make some friends, too. Last year, we designed our own chocolate business, did some engineering competitions, and saw the new tornado simulator!

IOWA

Program:	Iowa State University Offices of Precollegiate Programs for Gifted and Talented (OPPTAG)
Contact:	Maura Flaschner, Director, OPPTAG
Address:	Iowa State University 357 Carver Hall Ames, IA 50011-2060
Phone:	515-294-1772
Fax:	515-294-2592
E-mail:	opptag@iastate.edu
Web site:	http://www.opptag.iastate.edu
Program Type:	Academic Enrichment
Grade/Age Levels:	Grades 3–11
Description:	Iowa State University's OPPTAG offers academic enrichment through CY-TAG, Explorations!, and Adventures! During these programs students explore, observe, discover, question, scrutinize, evaluate, and ponder fascinating subjects such as art, astronomy, chemistry, computer science, history, literature, engineering, and psychology, along with other gifted students from Iowa, other states and across the globe. The program is for students interested in accelerated, fast-paced academic courses. *CY-TAG* will appeal to you if you are interested in accelerated, fast-paced, academic courses that address your individual needs and learning styles. You will be in class for approximately 100 hours of instructional time, which will cover a full year of high school or a semester of college material. *Explorations!* will appeal to you if you are intrigued by discovering new and exciting areas of study not traditionally taught in the high school curriculum. *Adventures!* will give younger students the opportunity to explore the worlds of science, ancient civilizations, math, art, literature, reading, and engineering led by qualified faculty.

Program:	Sande and Margo McNabb Internship Program
Contact:	Ms. Nina Grant, Director of Multicultural Programs
Address:	Sande and Margo McNabb Internship Program Iowa State University College of Agriculture 23 Curtiss Hall Ames, IA 50011-1050
Phone:	515-294-1701; 515-294-4519
Fax:	515-204-2844
E-mail:	nina1@iastate.edu
Web site:	http://www.ag.iastate.edu/student/Minority_ student_Programs-Summer_Internship_Program. html
Program Type:	Internships/Paid Positions
Grade/Age Levels:	Grades 9–12
Description:	For 6 weeks students are matched with faculty mentors and have the opportunity to conduct research in areas that interest them. Students will engage in research on a faculty-led team, participate in weekly seminars, social, cultural, and educational activities, tours on and off campus, and complete a final report. Students receive a stipend of $1,500 (stipends are subject to income tax), room and board, and are responsible for their own travel to and from Iowa State University. Students live on campus and have resident assistants available in the evenings and on the weekends for support.

KANSAS

Program:	**Exploring Science Technology & Engineering (EXCITE)**
Contact:	Ms. Susan Arnold Christian, Outreach Program Coordinator
Address:	Exploring Science Technology & Engineering Kansas State University 125 Seaton Hall Manhattan, KS 66506
Phone:	785-532-3395
Fax:	785-532-3349
E-mail:	susanac@ksu.edu
Web site:	http://www.k-state.edu/excite
Program Type:	Math, Sciences, Engineering, and Computer Science/Technology
Grade/Age Levels:	Grades 9–11
Description:	EXCITE! is designed to introduce young high school women to science, technology, engineering, and mathematics fields. EXCITE! is a year-round program that offers girls in grades 9–12 opportunities on and off campus. Girls entering grades 9 and 10 in the fall have the chance to participate in a 4-day hands-on residential science and engineering camp held on the Kansas State campus in Manhattan, KS. The EXCITE! workshop allows students to work closely with K-State faculty and undergraduate students. Participants also tour companies that employ scientists and engineers.

Program:	**The Center for Gifted Studies Summer Programs**
Contact:	Julia Roberts, Director
Address:	The Center for Gifted Studies Western Kentucky University 1906 College Heights Blvd #71031 Bowling Green KY 42101-1031
Phone:	270-745-6323
Fax:	270-745-6279
E-mail:	gifted@wku.edu
Web site:	http://www.wku.edu/gifted
Program Type:	Academic Enrichment
Grade/Age Levels:	Rising grades 7–9
Description:	The *Summer Camp for Academically Talented Middle School Students* (SCATS) provides an opportunity for students entering grades 7–9 to spend 2 weeks participating in myriad cultural, educational, and recreational activities. Students select four classes from dozens of choices. Students may be nonresidential or residential; residential campers live in an air-conditioned residence hall. Counselors supervise evening and weekend activities. The *Summer Program for Verbally and Mathematically Precocious Youth* (VAMPY) is a 3-week program for students in grades 7–10. Content areas include Ancient Civilizations, Genetics, Humanities, Nazi Germany and the Holocaust, and Spectra.

Program:	**ADVANCE Program for Young Scholars**
Contact:	Ms. Harriette Palmer, Assistant Director
Address:	ADVANCE Program for Young Scholars Northwestern State University NSU Box 5671 Natchitoches, LA 71497
Phone:	318-357-4500
Fax:	318-357-4547
E-mail:	palmerh@nsula.edu
Web site:	http://www.advanceprogram.org
Program Type:	Academic Enrichment
Grade/Age Levels:	Ages 12–17; Rising grades 8–12.
Description:	The ADVANCE Program for Young Scholars is a summer residential program that offers intensive, fast-paced courses in the humanities, mathematics, natural sciences, and computer science. Students selected to participate in ADVANCE enroll in one course during the 3-week term. By working with carefully selected instructors and teaching assistants, each student is given the opportunity to attain maximum academic growth. Classes are generally limited to 15 students. The residential life portion is an equally important aspect of the program and a wide array of extracurricular activities are offered each evening to encourage relaxation and socialization. ADVANCE is an affiliate program of the Duke University Talent Identification Program (TIP).

LOUISIANA

Program:	Camp Encore/Coda
Contact:	Ms. Jamie Saltman, Owner and Director
Address:	Camp Encore/Coda 32 Grassmere Rd. Brookline, MA 02467
Phone:	617-325-1541
Fax:	617-325-7278
E-mail:	jamie@encore-coda.com
Web site:	http://www.encore-coda.com
Program Type:	Fine, Performing, and Visual Arts
Grade/Age Levels:	Rising grade 9 and up
Description:	This summer camp is held in Sweden, ME each year and offers private musical training and ensemble training in everything from chamber music, to rock bands. High schoolers may be counselors in training and may also attend traditional program or the conservatory program for more intensive musical experience. The camp also includes traditional activities like arts and crafts, sports, canoeing, swimming, and field trips.

Summer Address:
    50 Encore/Coda Lane
    Sweden, ME 04040
    Phone: 207-647-3947
    Fax: 207-647-3259

Program:	**The Jackson Laboratory Summer Student Program**
Contact:	Dr. Jon Geiger, Summer Student Program
Address:	Education Office The Jackson Laboratory 600 Main St. Bar Harbor, ME 04609
Phone:	207-288-6250
Fax:	207-288-6051
E-mail:	summerstudent@jax.org
Web site:	http://www.jax.org/education/ssp.html
Program Type:	Internships/Paid Positions; Math, Sciences, Engineering, and Computer Science/Technology
Grade/Age Levels:	Grades 11–12
Description:	An internationally recognized center for mammalian genetic research, The Jackson Laboratory is an independent, nonprofit institution. Here, outstanding students conduct interdisciplinary biomedical research as apprentices in the laboratories of staff scientists. This program emphasizes methods of discovery and communication of new knowledge. Students also learn techniques, fundamentals, and ethics of biology, because these are essential in research. At the time of participation in the program, a high school student must have completed grade 11 or 12 and be at least 16 years old. Participants must be U.S. citizens or permanent residents. Students receive room and board and a stipend.

MAINE

Program:	**University of Maine Summer Youth Music**
Contact:	Bernie Duerkop Albert, Business Manager
Address:	University of Maine Summer Youth Music University of Maine School of Performing Arts 5788 Class of 1944 Hall Orono, ME 04469-5788
Phone:	207-581-4703
Fax:	207-581-4701
E-mail:	music@maine.edu
Web site:	http://www.umaine.edu/spa/navbarcamps.html
Program Type:	Fine, Performing, and Visual Arts
Grade/Age Levels:	Grades 6–12
Description:	The University of Maine Summer Youth Music program offers two levels of study: Junior Camp and Senior Camp. Junior Camp is for students entering grades 6–8. Each junior camper will participate in either symphonic band, concert band, or chorus. Additional ensembles will include jazz bands and musical theatre. Campers may also participate in chamber ensembles, music classes, master classes, and piano and guitar instruction. Senior Camp is for students entering grades 9–12. Each senior camper will participate in either symphonic band, concert band, or chorus. Additional ensembles will include jazz bands, combos, and musical theatre. Senior campers may also participate in jazz improvisation, small ensembles, chamber groups, music classes, master classes, and piano and guitar instruction.

Program:	The Workshops
Contact:	Mr. Charles Altschul, Executive Director
Address:	The Workshops P.O. Box 200 Rockport, ME 04856
Phone:	207-236-8581
Fax:	207-236-8519
E-mail:	info@theworkshops.com
Web site:	http://www.theworkshops.com/catalog/catalog.asp?schoolID=23
Program Type:	Fine, Performing, and Visual Arts
Grade/Age Levels:	Grades 9–12
Description:	Each summer a select group of high school students have the opportunity to spend one or two weeks studying and working in their chosen field of investigation: photography, film and video, film acting, or digital media. The campus experience allows these high school students the opportunity to work alongside the professionals, see their work, and listen to the world's most honored artists speak about their work and process. Young artists' workshops in photography, filmmaking, animation, and more are available to high school students throughout the summer—visit the Web site for a full listing of workshops and dates, or to download a course catalog.

MAINE

MARYLAND

Program:	**Center for Talented Youth (CTY) Summer Programs**
Contact:	Dr. Leo Ybarra, Executive Director
Address:	Johns Hopkins University Center for Talented Youth McAuley Hall 5801 Smith Ave., Ste 400 Baltimore, MD 21209
Phone:	410-735-4100
Fax:	410-735-6200
E-mail:	ctyinfo@jhu.edu
Web site:	http://www.cty.jhu.edu/summer/summer-programs.html
Program Type:	Academic Enrichment
Grade/Age Levels:	Grades 2–12
Description:	CTY summer program courses span a range of liberal arts disciplines, including language, history, writing, and the arts, as well as mathematics and science. All courses are challenging and are taught well above grade level. They cover a great deal of material and place emphasis on active learning and putting knowledge to use in independent and creative ways. Rather than assign grades, our instructors write detailed evaluations describing each student's progress and achievements in the course and outlining areas for further growth.

Program:	**Exploring Engineering at the University of Maryland (E2@UMD) Program**
Contact:	Ms. Alana Johnson, Coordinator, Women in Engineering
Address:	Exploring Engineering at the University of Maryland Program University of Maryland 1134F Glenn L. Martin Hall College Park, MD 20742
Phone:	301-405-3283
Fax:	301-314-9867
E-mail:	ajohns7@umd.edu
Web site:	http://www.eng.umd.edu/wie/precollege/e2umd.html
Program Type:	Math, Sciences, Engineering, and Computer Science/Technology
Grade/Age Levels:	Rising grades 11–12
Description:	This residential program, formerly the University of Maryland Summer Study in Engineering for High School Women, is a fun and exciting one-week camp introducing participants to engineering through hands-on activities, laboratory demonstrations, and seminars from faculty and other professional engineers. Participants will live on campus for one week and explore the world of engineering through fun hands-on activities, laboratory experiments, informative workshops, team LEGO challenges, and seminars with professional engineers. Students are exposed to female role models in engineering, introduced to other high school women with similar interests, and encouraged in their pursuit of engineering as a course of study in college.

Program:	**Java Passport Summer Workshop**
Contact:	Mr. Nelson Padua-Perez, Lecturer
Address:	Java Passport Summer Workshop University of Maryland Department of Computer Science A.V. Williams Bldg. 1129 College Park, MD 20742
Phone:	301-405-2672
E-mail:	nelson@cs.umd.edu
Web site:	http://www.cs.umd.edu/Passport
Program Type:	Math, Sciences, Engineering, and Computer Science/Technology
Grade/Age Levels:	Grades 7–12
Description:	The program is for middle and high school students interested in computer programming. The program includes an emphasis on encouraging females, Blacks, and Latinos to the fields of math and computer science. The program has three components: a spring component, a fall component, and a summer component. For the semester components (spring and fall), students attend classes on selected weekends. During the summer component, students attend classes daily during a 4-week period. This program is offered by the Department of Computer Science at the University of Maryland at College Park at no cost to the student (students are only responsible for transportation arrangements). Students must have at least a 3.4 GPA to apply.

Program:	**Marine Technology Society Summer Internship Program for High School Students**
Address:	Marine Technology Society 5565 Sterrett Pl., Ste. 108 Columbia, MD 21044
Phone:	410-884-5330
Fax:	410-884-9060
E-mail:	mtsmbrship@erols.com
Web site:	http://www.mts-sandiego.org/internship.php
Program Type:	Math, Sciences, Engineering, and Computer Science/Technology
Grade/Age Levels:	Grades 9–12
Description:	The San Diego Section of the Marine Technology Society has a summer internship program for high school students interested in the ocean professions. The San Diego MTS Program is a 6-week summer experience for motivated high school students hosted by one of MTS' corporate sponsors. Students get hands-on science and technology experiences, while building important scientific, technical, and employment skills under the direction of a workplace mentor. Students also receive a $1,620 stipend upon successful completion of the program. The International Marine Technology Society sponsors summer programs throughout the U. S. For example, the *Engineering Insights* camp at Texas A&M University is a residential 4-day summer program designed to give high school students with an interest in science, mathematics, and engineering an opportunity to explore engineering as a career.

Program:	Maryland Institute College of Art Pre-College Studio Residency Program
Address:	Pre-College Program Maryland Institute College of Art 1300 Mount Royal Ave. Baltimore, MD 21217
Phone:	410-225-2219
Fax:	410-225-2229
E-mail:	precollege@mica.edu
Web site:	http://www.mica.edu/PROGRAMS/cs/precollege
Program Type:	Fine, Performing, and Visual Arts
Grade/Age Levels:	Rising 11–12
Description:	This residential or commuter program offers the opportunity to earn three college credits, enhance your portfolio, and receive in-depth studio instruction, while experiencing college-level art study. Students receive workshop instruction in new media and art skills and complete an art history seminar. Full and partial scholarships are available. MICA's home base of Baltimore is at the heart of the New York–Washington, D.C. art corridor. Saturday trips during the residency program will let you explore nationally and internationally recognized art museums.

Program:	**Stepping Stones to Your Future**
Contact:	Fran Lee, Camp Coordinator
Address:	Stepping Stones to Your Future University of Maryland 1134F Glenn L. Martin Hall College Park, MD 20742
Phone:	301-405-0315
Fax:	301-314-9867
E-mail:	franlee@umd.edu
Web site:	http://www.engr.umd.edu/wie/precollege/stepstone.html
Program Type:	Math, Sciences, Engineering, and Computer Science/Technology
Grade/Age Levels:	Rising grades 7–8
Description:	Stepping Stones to Your Future is an annual summer engineering camp for rising seventh and eighth graders, offered by the University of Maryland, College Park. This one-week commuter camp is an excellent opportunity for young men and women who are interested in science and engineering to work with current University of Maryland students on a variety of fun and hands-on engineering activities.

Program:	**Summer Institute in Science, Technology, Engineering, and Research (SISTER)**
Contact:	Dr. Antoinette Wells
Address:	Summer Institute in Science, Technology, Engineering, and Research NASA/Goddard Space Flight Center Education Office Code 120 Greenbelt, MD 20771
Phone:	301-286-7262
E-mail:	Antoinette.C.Wells@nasa.gov
Web site:	http://education.gsfc.nasa.gov/pages/sister.html
Program Type:	Academic Enrichment
Grade/Age Levels:	Rising grade 8
Description:	SISTER, the Summer Institute in Science, Technology, Engineering, and Research at NASA Goddard Space Flight Center, is a 5-day, nonresidential program for girls entering the eighth grade. Participants explore careers in math, science, and technology through a variety of activities with NASA Goddard Space Flight Center's women scientists, engineers, mathematicians, researchers, and technicians. The program is held the fourth week in June and is open to female applicants with at least a B average in math and/or science. The program is free; participants are responsible for travel, accommodations, transportation, and lunch.

Program:	**Summer Internship in Biomedical Research**
Address:	Summer Internship in Biomedical Research National Institute of Health (NIH) 2 Center Dr. MSC 0240 Bethesda, MD 20892-0240
Phone:	800-445-8283
Fax:	301-402-0483
Web site:	http://www.training.nih.gov/student/sip/info.asp
Program Type:	Internships/Paid Positions
Grade/Age Levels:	Ages 16 and up
Description:	The Summer Internship Program (SIP) at the NIH provides an opportunity to spend the summer working side-by-side with some of the leading scientists in the world in an environment devoted exclusively to biomedical research. Students 16 years of age or older, who are U.S. citizens or permanent residents, and are currently enrolled at least half-time in high school or an accredited U.S. college or university are eligible to apply. Students who have been accepted into a college or university may also apply. The stipends for trainees are adjusted yearly, with supplements for prior experience.

MARYLAND

Program:	University of Maryland Jump Start Program
Contact:	Dr. Kaci Thompson, Director
Address:	Jump Start Program University of Maryland College of Chemical and Life Sciences 1313 Symons Hall College Park, MD 20742
Phone:	301-405-3353
E-mail:	HHMI@umd.edu
Web site:	http://www.chemlife.umd.edu/hhmi/jumpstart
Program Type:	Math, Sciences, Engineering, and Computer Science/Technology
Grade/Age Levels:	Grades 11 and up
Description:	This weeklong science immersion program allows commuter students to learn about the research process while working in the university's biology laboratories. Past programs have focused on forensic science, biomedical science, biotechnology, and animal physiology and behavior. Applications must be postmarked by March 15.

Program:	**Adventures in Veterinary Medicine (AVM)**
Address:	Tufts University Cummings School of Veterinary Medicine 200 Westboro Rd. North Grafton, MA 01536
Phone:	508-839-7962
Fax:	508-839-7952
E-mail:	AVM@tufts.edu
Web site:	http://www.tufts.edu/vet/avm/high.html
Program Type:	Academic Enrichment
Grade/Age Levels:	Grades 9–12
Description:	Have you ever wondered what it would be like to be a veterinarian? AVM is a career exploration program. Students attend lectures from the clinical faculty, gain practical information about applying to and attending veterinary school, engage in hands-on activities with animals, and are assigned to clinical rotations where they shadow fourth-year students in the hospital.

MASSACHUSETTS

MASSACHUSETTS

Program:	**Audubon Expedition Institute (AEI)**
Contact:	Ms. Paige Manning, Assistant Director
Address:	Audubon Expedition Institute Lesley University Advising and Student Services 29 Everett St. Cambridge, MA 02138
Phone:	888-287-2234; 800-999-1959 ext. 8489
Web site:	http://www.getonthebus.org
Program Type:	Gap Year/Study Abroad/International Travel
Grade/Age Levels:	Grades 13–20
Description:	The Audubon Expedition Institute at Lesley University is an academically rigorous alternative to traditional colleges and universities for undergraduate or graduate students pursuing a deeper ecological understanding of environmental education, leadership, and advocacy. Our goal is to create experiential learning communities that inspire informed and compassionate ecological leadership. Interested in sustainable living? The Audubon Expedition Institute at Lesley University offers a 3-week summer Sustainable Practices Program. Earn six undergraduate credits exploring sustainable living in rural Maine. Put into practice ecological concepts and alternative solutions you may have heard of, but never had the chance to try.

Program:	Bard College at Simon's Rock Young Writers Workshop
Contact:	Dr. Jamie Hutchinson, Director
Address:	Young Writers Workshop Bard College at Simon's Rock 84 Alford Rd. Great Barrington, MA 01230
Phone:	413-528-7231
Fax:	413-528-7365
E-mail:	jamieh@simons-rock.edu
Web site:	http://www.simons-rock.edu/young_writers
Program Type:	Academic Enrichment
Grade/Age Levels:	Grades 9–12
Description:	The Young Writers Workshop was established at Simon's Rock in 1983 and is modeled after Bard College's innovative precollege writing program. Each year 78–84 students are selected to participate. Unlike conventional workshops in creative or expository writing, Simon Rock's 3-week program focuses on using informal, playful expressive writing as a way to strengthen skills of language and thinking. Out of this informal writing, using techniques of peer response, students develop more polished pieces, from poems and stories, to reflective essays. Classes are small and emphasize an atmosphere of trust and collaboration. Emphasis is given to discovering one's personal voice as a writer. Students have the opportunity to attend plays, concerts, and other cultural activities that are part of summer life in the Berkshires.

MASSACHUSETTS

Program:	**Boston Architectural College (BAC) High School Summer Academy**
Address:	Boston Architectural College Continuing Education Department 320 Newbury St. Boston, MA 02115
Phone:	617-585-0101
Fax:	617-585-0121
E-mail:	summer@the-bac.edu
Web site:	http://www.the-bac.edu/summer
Program Type:	Academic Enrichment
Grade/Age Levels:	Grades 10 and up
Description:	BAC Summer Academy is an exciting career exploration program for high school students who have a strong interest in architecture or design professions. Throughout the 4-week program, students experience the field of design through hands-on projects, interactive learning, and educational field trips. As part of their experience, students collaborate on a team venture to design and build a full-scale project. At the conclusion of the program, students' work will be exhibited at the BAC. Participants leave the program with new items for their portfolio and a stronger sense of whether to pursue a career in the field of design. Scholarships are available based on financial need, as well as through the Houseman/Kirkham Fund established to promote diversity in the design professions. Houseman Scholars attend BAC Summer Academy free of charge, may potentially be invited back the following summer to mentor new students, and will be eligible for a substantial scholarship to the Boston Architectural College to pursue a bachelor's degree in architecture, interior design, or landscape architecture.

Program:	**Boston University Summer Programs**
Contact:	Ms. Alexandra Adams, Assistant Director
Address:	Boston University High School Honors Program 755 Commonwealth Ave., Room 105 Boston, MA 02215
Phone:	617-353-1378
Fax:	617-353-5532
E-mail:	buhssumr@bu.edu
Web site:	http://www.bu.edu/summer/ program_high_school_students
Program Type:	Academic Enrichment
Grade/Age Levels:	Grade 12
Description:	The *Research Internship Program in Science and Engineering*, held at Boston University for 6 weeks during the summer, offers internships in research settings to highly talented students who are entering their senior year in high school. These students join active research groups in physics, engineering, astronomy, chemistry, and biology. Faculty members and their research staff serve as mentors to the interns, providing the guidance and background needed for them to become active members of a research team.
	Boston University also offers a 6-week general honors summer program for students wanting to earn eight BU credits in two academic courses of their choice. Visit the above Web site for more information.
	The BU 2-week *Summer Challenge Program* allows high school students who will be entering their sophomore, junior, or senior year to preview college life and coursework. Students explore two subject areas of their choice in specially designed, noncredit seminars.

MASSACHUSETTS

Program:	**Boston University Summer Theater Institute**
Contact:	Paolo DiFabio, Assistant Director
Address:	Boston University Summer Theater Institute College of Fine Arts 855 Commonwealth Ave., 4th Floor Boston, MA 02215
Phone:	617-353-3340
Fax:	617-353-4663
E-mail:	arts@bu.edu
Web site:	http://www.bu.edu/cfa/theatre/sti/index.htm
Program Type:	Fine, Performing, and Visual Arts
Grade/Age Levels:	Grades 10–12
Description:	The Boston University Summer Theatre Institute is a 5-week program for serious and mature high school students. It is designed for those who wish to test their interests and abilities in a professional training environment. In this program, students develop confidence and technique, acquire insight and expertise, and learn to meet intellectual and artistic challenges. College credit is also available.

Program:	**Camp Reach and Camp Strive**
Address:	Camp Reach Worcester Polytechnic Institute 100 Institute Rd. Worcester, MA 01609-2280
Phone:	508-831-5819
Fax:	508-831-5818
E-mail:	reach@wpi.edu; diversity@wpi.edu
Web site:	http://www.wpi.edu/Admin/Women/Girls/Reach; http://www.wpi.edu/Admin/Diversity/k12/Strive
Program Type:	Math, Sciences, Engineering, & Computer Science/Technology
Grade/Age Levels:	Rising grades 7 and up
Description:	*Camp Reach* is a summer residential program for girls in Massachusetts who have completed the sixth grade and who are interested in learning more about careers in engineering and technology. *Camp Strive* is a hands-on exploration of engineering, math, and science, for Black, Hispanic, and Native American students in grades 9–12. Students will be able to learn more about potential careers in these areas by engaging in labs facilitated by a dedicated team of WPI faculty and students. Scholarships are available.

MASSACHUSETTS

Program:	The Forsyth Institute Educational Outreach Program
Contact:	Dr. Martin Taubman, Program Director
Address:	Educational Outreach Program The Forsyth Institute 140 The Fenway Boston, MA 02115-3799
Phone:	617-892-8314
Fax:	617-262-5200
E-mail:	mtaubman@forsyth.org
Web site:	http://www.forsyth.org/forsyth.asp?pg=100068
Program Type:	Internships/Paid Positions
Grade/Age Levels:	Grades 9–12
Description:	This summer program offers an 8-week paid internship, during which students are paired with Forsyth researchers as mentors. Over the summer, the interns learn basic laboratory techniques and participate in ongoing research projects. At the end of the program, students present scientific posters describing their findings. Students may continue working on their projects during the academic year. Student interns spend the summer in a productive and enriching environment. For these underrepresented youth, the Educational Outreach Program not only is often their first "real" job, but also may be their first step toward a future career path filled with challenges and achievements.

MASSACHUSETTS

Program:	**Genesis at Brandeis University**
Contact:	Bradley Solmsen, Director
Address:	Genesis at Brandeis University Brandeis University South St. MS 037 Waltham, MA 02454-9110
Phone:	781-736-8416
Fax:	781-736-8122
E-mail:	genesis@brandeis.edu
Web site:	http://www.brandeis.edu/genesis
Program Type:	Academic Enrichment; Leadership/Service/Volunteer
Grade/Age Levels:	Rising grade 11 and up
Description:	Genesis integrates Jewish studies, the arts, humanities, and social action in this unique program. In 2007, courses included studies of world religions; Jewish law; theater arts; Judaism and journalism; and Jewish values, humanity, and the environment. The program lasts 4 weeks and includes field trips and community service. Tuition is subsidized and scholarships are available.

MASSACHUSETTS

Program:	Harvard: Project Success
Contact:	Dr. Sheila Nutt, Director, Educational Outreach
Address:	Project Success Harvard University Minority Faculty Development Program 164 Longwood Ave., 2nd Floor Boston, MA 02115-5818
Phone:	617-432-4634
E-mail:	sheila_nutt@hms.harvard.edu
Web site:	http://www.mfdp.med.harvard.edu/k12/project_success/index.htm
Program Type:	Internships/Paid Positions
Grade/Age Levels:	Grades 9–12
Description:	Project Success targets Boston and Cambridge minority high school students to participate in mentored summer research internships at Harvard Medical School and its affiliated institutions. The program is augmented by seminars and workshops given by faculty and administrators, site visits, a SAT preparation course, and career guidance counseling. Students must be a high school student, particularly a student from an underrepresented racial or ethnic background and/or from a disadvantaged background, and reside in Boston or Cambridge to participate. The program includes paid "hands-on" research positions for 8 weeks, from June through August; summer discussion series; seminars with researchers and physicians; site visits to hospitals and biotechnology firms; computer training; development of writing and speaking skills; academic year seminars and special programs; assigned mentors and research advisors; information about the college application process; and career counseling.

Program:	**Harvard Secondary School Program**
Contact:	Mr. William Holinger, Director
Address:	Harvard Secondary School Program Harvard University 51 Brattle St. Cambridge, MA 02138
Phone:	617-495-3192
Fax:	617-496-4525
E-mail:	ssp@hudce.harvard.edu
Web site:	http://www.ssp.harvard.edu
Program Type:	Academic Enrichment
Grade/Age Levels:	Rising grade 10 and up
Description:	Students can choose from 200 courses offered at Harvard. They have a choice of 4-credit courses or one 8-credit course. Students will have access to a distinguished faculty, well-equipped labs, exceptional museums, and the largest university library system in the world. They will live and learn with students of many ages from all areas of the United States and more than 90 countries. Room and board is available. See Web site and catalog for course listing.

MASSACHUSETTS

Program:	Mathcamp
Contact:	Dr. Mira Bernstein, Executive Director
Address:	Canada/USA Mathcamp Mathematics Foundation of America 129 Hancock St. Cambridge, MA 02139
Phone:	617-812-6339
Fax:	617-812-6339
E-mail:	mc-info@mathcamp.org
Web site:	http://www.mathcamp.org
Program Type:	Math, Sciences, Engineering, and Computer Science/Technology
Grade/Age Levels:	Ages 13–18
Description:	Mathcamp is an intensive 5-week summer program for high school students interested in mathematics. Our goals are to inspire and motivate these students by introducing them to the beauty and variety of advanced mathematics; to impart valuable knowledge and skills for the pursuit of mathematics in high school, university, and beyond; and to provide a supportive and fun environment for interaction among students who love mathematics. The location varies each year; the 2008 location is Reed College in Portland, OR.

Program:	**Minds, Matter, and Medicine in the 21st Century**
Contact:	Ms. Dawn Sanders, Summer Science Program Coordinator
Address:	Clark University Admissions Office 950 Main St. Worcester, MA 01610-1477
Phone:	508-793-7431; 800-462-5275
Fax:	508-793-8821
E-mail:	dsanders@clarku.edu
Web site:	http://www.clarku.edu/admissions/specialprograms/summerscienceprogram/index.cfm
Program Type:	Math, Sciences, Engineering, and Computer Science/Technology
Grade/Age Levels:	Grade 12
Description:	Are there cures for cancer, Alzheimer's or even old age? Are computers and minds really that different? What is the universe made of, how did it come to be, and what is its future? Are you intrigued by these questions? If so, Clark University's summer program, Minds, Matter, and Medicine in the 21st Century, is for you. For 3 weeks in July, Clark's campus buzzes with high school seniors interested in the sciences. The course is team-taught by five Clark faculty members from various departments. The program offers college credit, room, and board at absolutely no cost. It will provide an opportunity for students to join our faculty in exploring some of the hottest topics in science and math in daily discussions and laboratory workshops.

MASSACHUSETTS

Program:	**MIT Women's Technology Program**
Contact:	Ms. Cynthia Skier, Director
Address:	Women's Technology Program Massachusetts Institute of Technology MIT Room 38-491 77 Massachusetts Ave. Cambridge, MA 02139
Phone:	617-253-5580
E-mail:	wtp@mit.edu
Web site:	http://wtp.mit.edu
Program Type:	Math, Sciences, Engineering, and Computer Science/Technology; Leadership/Service/Volunteer
Grade/Age Levels:	Grade 11
Description:	The MIT Women's Technology Program (WTP) is a 4-week summer academic and residential experience where female high school students explore engineering and computer science through hands-on classes, labs, and team-based projects in their summer after 11th grade. Students attend WTP in either: Electrical Engineering and Computer Science (EECS) or Mechanical Engineering (ME). Courses are taught by female MIT graduate students. Students must apply by February 1 of their junior year to attend the following summer.

Program:	**The Program in Mathematics for Young Scientists (PROMYS)**
Contact:	Professor Glenn Stevens, Director
Address:	The Program in Mathematics for Young Scientists Boston University Department of Mathematics 111 Cummington St. Boston, MA 02215
Phone:	617-353-2563
Fax:	617-353-8100
E-mail:	promys@math.bu.edu
Web site:	http://www.promys.org http://math.bu.edu/people/promys
Program Type:	Math, Sciences, Engineering, and Computer Science/Technology
Grade/Age Levels:	Grades 9–12
Description:	PROMYS is a 6-week summer program at Boston University designed to encourage motivated high school students (grades 9–12, who are age 14 or older) to explore the creative world of mathematics in a supportive community of peers, counselors, research mathematicians, and visiting scientists.

MASSACHUSETTS

Program:	**SEARCH at Mount Holyoke College**
Contact:	Drs. Charlene and Jim Morrow, Directors
Address:	SEARCH Mount Holyoke College 50 College St. South Hadley, MA 01075-1441
Phone:	413-538-2608
Fax:	413-538-2002
E-mail:	search@mtholyoke.edu
Web site:	http://www.mtholyoke.edu/proj/search
Program Type:	Math, Sciences, Engineering, and Computer Science/Technology
Grade/Age Levels:	Grades 8–11
Description:	SEARCH is a 4-week residential and commuter program for young women who are adventurous, who have done well in high school mathematics, and who would like to experience a different aspect of the world of mathematics. Prospective students should have a strong background in college preparatory mathematics and a strong desire to investigate problems in small groups of students with a faculty leader-facilitator. SEARCH is designed to give the feel of the world and work of mathematics.

Program:	**Smith College Summer Science and Engineering Program**
Contact:	Dr. Gail Scordilis, Director
Address:	Summer Science and Engineering Program Smith College Educational Outreach Clark Hall Northampton, MA 01063
Phone:	413-585-3060
Fax:	413-585-3068
E-mail:	gscordil@smith.edu
Web site:	http://www.smith.edu/summerprograms/ssep
Program Type:	Math, Sciences, Engineering, and Computer Science/Technology
Grade/Age Levels:	Rising grades 9–12
Description:	This 4-week program is geared toward exceptional young women with strong interests in science, engineering, and medicine. Students take two 2-week science research courses of their choice, including lectures, field work, and science experiments. In 2007, research courses included studies on exercise, robotics, genetics, and astronomical imaging. Financial aid is available.

MASSACHUSETTS

Program:	**Student Challenge Awards Program (SCAP)**
Address:	Student Challenge Awards Program Earthwatch Institute International Headquarters 3 Clock Tower Pl., Ste. 100 P.O. Box 75 Maynard, MA 01754
Phone:	978-450-1264; 800-776-0188
Fax:	978-450-1288
E-mail:	SCAP@earthwatch.org
Web site:	http://www.earthwatch.org
Program Type:	Internships/Paid Positions
Grade/Age Levels:	Ages 16–18
Description:	The Student Challenge Awards Program offers students ages 16–18 gifted in the arts and humanities an opportunity to spend 2–3 intensive weeks during the summer at a scientific research station. The aim is to excite the students' imagination, expand their potential, and stimulate their curiosity about science and technology. SCAP is a competitive fellowship program that rewards creative thinkers and risk takers. The program is funded by an outside donor and implemented by Earthwatch. This program is for students without prior experience helping a scientist conduct research. Students are assigned to sites selected by Earthwatch for the quality of research and educational commitment of the scientific staff. Visit our listed Web site for location and date information.

Program:	**Suffolk University Residential Summer Institutes**
Contact:	Mr. Curtis Hoover, Program Director
Address:	Residential Summer Institutes Suffolk University 150 Tremont St. Boston, MA 02111
Phone:	617-305-2500
Fax:	617-305-2504
E-mail:	summerprograms@suffolk.edu
Web site:	http://www.suffolk.edu/summerinstitutes
Program Type:	Academic Enrichment
Grade/Age Levels:	Grades 9–12
Description:	The Suffolk University Residential Summer Institute's 2-week intensive summer experiences for high school sophomores and juniors are a great opportunity to have a thrilling academic and cultural experience in the heart of downtown Boston. Students can experience college life while still in high school and can choose from workshops and institutes such as the Politics and Public Service Institute, Student Leadership and Service Learning Institute, GLBT Awareness Institute, Business Organization and Leadership Institute, Institute for the Empowerment of Women of Color, Screenwriting and Video Production Institute, Improv Comedy Workshop, and Institute for an Understanding of World Religions and Spirituality.

MASSACHUSETTS

Program:	**SummerMath at Mount Holyoke College**
Contact:	Drs. Charlene and James Morrow, Directors
Address:	SummerMath Mount Holyoke College 50 College St. South Hadley, MA 01075-1441
Phone:	413-538-2608
Fax:	413-538-2002
E-mail:	summermath@mtholyoke.edu
Web site:	http://www.mtholyoke.edu/proj/summermath/ smhome.html
Program Type:	Math, Sciences, Engineering, and Computer Science/Technology
Grade/Age Levels:	Grades 8–11
Description:	SummerMath engages young women in the process of problem solving and learning mathematics. During the 4-week residential and commuter programs, students take a mathematics class, a computer programming class, and two 2-week workshops on topics such as economics, architecture, robotics, anatomy, and statistics. The SummerMath program at Mount Holyoke College is designed for high school girls who have excelled in mathematics and would like to see a different aspect of the mathematical world.

Program:	WUNDERS: Women, Understanding New Dimensions in Engineering Related Science
Address:	Worcester Polytechnic Institute WUNDERS 100 Institute Rd. Worcester, MA 01609-2280
Phone:	831-831-5819
Fax:	508-881-5818
E-mail:	wunders@wpi.edu
Web site:	http://www.wpi.edu/Admin/Women/Girls/WUNDERS
Program Type:	Math, Sciences, Engineering, and Computer Science/Technology
Grade/Age Levels:	Grades 9–12
Description:	WUNDERS is a hands-on exploration of engineering, math, and science for young women. This residential, 10-day program includes lab workshops, such as comparing water from different sources and building robots that respond to sound, along with engineering design projects.

MASSACHUSETTS

Program:	**You GO Girl!**
Contact:	Ms. Amy Fitzgerald, Outreach Coordinator
Address:	You GO Girl! Massachusetts Institute of Technology Edgerton Center 77 Massachusetts Ave., Room 4-406 Cambridge, MA 02139-4307
Phone:	617-253-7931
Fax:	617-253-1535
E-mail:	amyfitz@mit.edu
Web site:	http://web.mit.edu/edgerton/outreach/ygg.html
Program Type:	Math, Sciences, Engineering, and Computer Science/Technology
Grade/Age Levels:	Grade 9
Description:	You GO Girl! is a 4-day summer commuter program that runs annually in August on the MIT campus. The program is designed for girls only, and only for those going into ninth grade the September following camp. The program combines an introduction to a variety of science and engineering strands, as well as high school preparation courses.

MASSACHUSETTS

Program:	Young Artist Residency Program
Contact:	Kerri Fisher, Coordinator of Extended Programs
Address:	Lesley University Art Institute of Boston 700 Beacon St. Boston, MA 02215
Phone:	617-585-6724; 617-585-6729; 800-773-0494 ext. 6724
Fax:	617-585-6721
E-mail:	kfisher3@aiboston.edu
Web site:	http://web.lesley.edu
Program Type:	Fine, Performing, and Visual Arts; Academic Enrichment
Grade/Age Levels:	Grades 11–12
Description:	The Summer Young Artist Residency Program is available in July for a limited number of students who will be entering their junior or senior year of high school. The Art Institute of Boston has established the YAP program to provide access to AIB's extensive Summer Pre-College Program, as well as help students test out an art college environment. Six college credits are awarded after successful completion of the residency program. Accepted students choose a full schedule of courses from the summer precollege program and live in the Lesley University residences on the Cambridge campus.

Program:	**American Youth Foundation Leadership Conferences**
Address:	American Youth Foundation Leadership Conferences 8845 W. Garfield Rd. Shelby, MI 49455
Phone:	231-861-2262
Fax:	231-861-5244
E-mail:	leadershipconferences@ayf.com
Web site:	http://www.ayf.com/youth-development-leadership-conference.asp
Program Type:	Leadership/Service/Volunteer
Grade/Age Levels:	Ages 15–20
Description:	Are you a high school student looking for an opportunity to enhance your leadership skills, develop your personal effectiveness, and focus on living a balanced life? Participants from across the nation gather together on the beautiful shores of Lake Michigan for an intensive weeklong program focusing on personal effectiveness, effectiveness in groups, openness to diversity, and social responsibility. The foundation also offers two summer camps in Shelby, MI, and Center Tuftonboro, NH.

Program:	Camp CAEN (Computer Aided Engineering Network)
Contact:	Ms. Ann Gordon, Camp Director
Address:	Camp CAEN University of Michigan College of Engineering 2318 Duderstadt Center 2281 Bonisteel Blvd. Ann Arbor, MI 48109-2094
Phone:	734-936-8039
Fax:	734-615-3011
E-mail:	campcaen@umich.edu
Web site:	http://www.engin.umich.edu/caen/campcaen
Program Type:	Math, Sciences, Engineering, and Computer Science/Technology
Grade/Age Levels:	Ages 10–17
Description:	From the engineering student labs to an immersive Virtual Reality CAVE, no other computer camps offer the variety and depth of technology available at Camp CAEN. High-tech is here and students are invited to discover the endless possibilities awaiting them at the University of Michigan College of Engineering Summer Computer Camp CAEN. Classes include Java programming, C++ programming, C# programming, game development, artificial intelligence (AI), Web site development, Flash animation, 3D modeling and rendering, virtual reality, and more!

MICHIGAN

Program:	**Engineering Exploration With WIMS Technology**
Contact:	Mr. Drew Kim, Recruiting and K–12 Outreach
Address:	Engineering Exploration With WIMS Technology Michigan State University College of Engineering 3410 Engineering Building East Lansing, MI 48824-1226
Phone:	517-355-5113
Fax:	517-353-7282
E-mail:	kima@egr.msu.edu
Web site:	http://www.egr.msu.edu/egr/programs/precollege/wimsforteens/index.php
Program Type:	Math, Sciences, Engineering, and Computer Science/Technology
Grade/Age Levels:	Grades 7–9
Description:	This 4-day commuter program is dedicated to enriching the engineering experience for those who are interested and motivated to choose careers in science, math, and engineering, specifically in the area of Wireless Integrated Microsystems (WIMS) technology.
	Students will work on group projects to develop their own electronic thermometer and robotic fish.

MICHIGAN

Program:	**Interlochen Arts Camp**
Address:	Interlochen Center for the Arts Admissions Office P.O. Box 199 Interlochen, MI 49643-0199
Phone:	231-276-7472; 800-681-5912
Fax:	231-276-7464
E-mail:	admissions@interlochen.org
Web site:	http://www.interlochen.org/camp
Program Type:	Fine, Performing, and Visual Arts
Grade/Age Levels:	Grades 3–12
Description:	Each summer, more than 2,100 of the world's most talented and motivated young people come to Interlochen to live, learn, and perform with an unparalleled group of peers and educators. Founded in 1928, Interlochen is the first and foremost camp of its kind, offering both visual and performing arts camp programs for student artists in grades 3–12. This residential program provides study in creative writing, dance, general arts, motion picture arts, music, theatre arts, and visual arts.

MICHIGAN

MICHIGAN

Program:	**Kettering University Summer Programs**
Contact:	Ms. Deborah Stewart, Program Coordinator or Mr. Ricky Brown, Director of Pre-College Programs
Address:	Kettering University 1700 W. Third Ave., Room 3-100 CC Flint, MI 48504-4898
Phone:	810-762-9679; 800-955-4464 ext. 9679
Fax:	810-762-9582
E-mail:	LITE@kettering.edu
Web site:	http://www.kettering.edu/lite; http://www.kettering.edu/kampkettering; http://www.kettering.edu/precollege
Program Type:	Math, Sciences, Engineering, and Computer Science/Technology
Grade/Age Levels:	Grades 6–12
Description:	*LITE* is a 2-week residential program meant to introduce girls who will be entering grade 12 to engineering specialties. Participants will learn to design everyday products that make a profound impact, such as air bags, artificial limbs, and car seats. Thirty-six selected participants from across the country will experience classes and labs taught by Kettering faculty in exciting subjects. *Academically Interested Minorities* (AIM) is a 5-week, free, residential summer program designed to help students of color make a successful transition from high school to college. *Kamp Kettering* is a one-week summer enrichment program for girls who have just completed the sixth and seventh grades and are interested in science, math, engineering, and technology.

Program:	**Math, Science, and Technology at Michigan State University**
Contact:	Ms. Kathee McDonald, Director
Address:	Math, Science, and Technology at Michigan State University
	Michigan State University
	186 Bessey Hall
	East Lansing, MI 48824
Phone:	517-432-2129
Fax:	517-353-6464
E-mail:	mcdon288@msu.edu
Web site:	http://www.msu.edu/~gifted/mst/mst.htm
Program Type:	Math, Sciences, Engineering, and Computer Science/Technology, Academic Enrichment
Grade/Age Levels:	Grades 8–9
Description:	Called MST at MSU, this 2-week summer residential program is designed specifically for academically talented students who have just completed seventh or eighth grade. The challenging coursework provides enrichment but does not duplicate or accelerate coursework of a typical school curriculum. In the program, students investigate real-world problems using science, math, and technology. The program will stimulate them to learn about new developments in career fields where these subjects are important. Courses are taught by MSU professors using interdisciplinary strategies. Students are housed on campus, where they will enjoy social, athletic, and extracurricular activities with other students from Michigan and other states.
	Visit the Web site for more eligibility and application information.

MICHIGAN

MICHIGAN

Program:	**Michigan State University Engineering Summer Programs**
Contact:	Mr. Drew Kim, Recruiting and K–12 Outreach
Address:	Michigan State University College of Engineering 3410 Engineering Building East Lansing, MI 48824-1226
Phone:	517-355-5113; 517-353-7282
Fax:	517-355-2288
E-mail:	kima@egr.msu.edu
Web site:	http://www.egr.msu.edu/egr/programs/precollege/ wimsforteens/index.php
Program Type:	Math, Sciences, Engineering, and Computer Science/Technology
Grade/Age Levels:	Grades 4–12
Description:	In addition to the Wireless Integrated MicroSystems (WIMS) for Teens summer program (p. 188), Michigan State University also offers the following programs:

- The *Engineering Exploration: LEGO Robotics to WIMS Program* is a one-week commuter program. It is designed to explore various engineering fields and focuses on problem identification, team-building, communication, problem solving, programming, research methods, presentation, and competition.
- The *Women in Engineering* (WIE) residential program hosts 26 high school women (currently in grades 10–12) who are given the opportunity to explore a variety of engineering fields, and to participate in practical, interactive, and theory-based application experiences. Designed to encourage high school women to consider engineering as a career option. The program requires a 3.2 or higher grade point average or individual ranking in the top 15% of cohort class.

Program:	**Michigan Technological University Summer Youth Program**
Contact:	Youth Programs Coordinator
Address:	Summer Youth Program Michigan Technological University Youth Programs Office Alumni House 1400 Townsend Dr. Houghton, MI 49931-1295
Phone:	888-PRECOLLEGE
Fax:	906-487-3101
E-mail:	syp@mtu.edu
Web site:	http://youthprograms.mtu.edu
Program Type:	Academic Enrichment
Grade/Age Levels:	Grades 9–11
Description:	The Michigan Technological University Summer Youth Program (SYP) will introduce you to careers and allow you to develop new skills through laboratory, classroom, and field experiences. The SYP curriculum offers more than 90 sections of explorations scheduled over multiple weeks, with the total enrollment limited to about 1,200 students. An exploration is an intensive weeklong look at a particular field or area of interest and is offered in seven different categories designed to introduce you to a world of opportunities. You will spend approximately 30 hours investigating your area of interest through classroom activities, hands-on laboratory exercises, field trips, and discussions with your instructors and other students. This is a residential program. There are some special programs for middle school students.

MICHIGAN

Program:	**Sustainable Energy Pre-College Program**
Contact:	Ms. Virginia Hill, Program Coordinator
Address:	Sustainable Energy Pre-College Program Kettering University 1700 W. Third Ave. Flint, MI 48504-4898
Phone:	810-762-9873
Fax:	810-762-7492
E-mail:	vhill@kettering.edu
Web site:	http://www.kettering.edu/futurestudents/ undergraduate/sustainable_energy_precollege.jsp
Program Type:	Math, Sciences, Engineering, and Computer Science/Technology
Grade/Age Levels:	Grades 9–12
Description:	Students will have fun exploring:

- how fuel cells work;
- the different ways of powering fuel cells;
- how fuel cells can be used to power homes, cars, and buses;
- how to build a fuel cell car and wind turbine from a kit (take-home project);
- how solar, hydro, and wind power can be used; and
- careers in sustainable energy.

The program will provide hands-on educational experience including exhibits, laboratory, and classroom activities, as well as a fun field trip.

Program:	WIE: Women in Engineering Workshop
Contact:	Youth Programs Coordinator
Address:	WIE: Women in Engineering Workshop Michigan Technological University Youth Programs Office Alumni House 1400 Townsend Dr. Houghton, MI 49931-1295
Phone:	888-PRECOLLEGE
Fax:	906-487-3101
E-mail:	yp@mtu.edu
Web site:	http://youthprograms.mtu.edu/wie/index.html
Program Type:	Math, Sciences, Engineering, and Computer Science/Technology
Grade/Age Levels:	Grades 9–11
Description:	The Women in Engineering Workshop (WIE) is a one-week experience which allows young women who are academically talented in mathematics and/or science the opportunity to investigate careers in engineering and science. Courses will be taught by practicing women engineers from industry and the government, educators, and university faculty. Each session includes a laboratory experience, a team engineering project, and time to interact formally and informally with role models and talented peers. Students will get to investigate engineering careers, as well as other related disciplines.

MICHIGAN

Program:	**Carleton College Summer Writing Program**
Address:	Summer Writing Program Carleton College Office of Summer Academic Programs One N. College St. Northfield, MN 55057
Phone:	507-646-4038; 866-767-2275 (toll-free)
Fax:	507-646-4540
E-mail:	swp@carleton.edu; summer@carleton.edu
Web site:	http://apps.carleton.edu/campus/SAP/writing
Program Type:	Academic Enrichment
Grade/Age Levels:	Grades 11 and up
Description:	Every summer, more than 80 high school juniors gather on the campus of Carleton College for 3 weeks of intensive writing instruction, fun, and friendship. Emphasizing a writing process approach, this program helps students learn to compose academic papers that are similar to those they will write in college. Students read both contemporary and traditional literature, which then become the focus of their essays. The program is for college-bound students in their junior year of high school.

Program:	**Carleton Liberal Arts Experience (CLAE)**
Contact:	Mr. Todd Olson, Director of CLAE
Address:	Carleton College 100 S. College St. Northfield, MN 55057
Phone:	866-767-2275
Fax:	507-646-4526
E-mail:	clae@carleton.edu
Web site:	http://apps.carleton.edu/summer/clae
Program Type:	Academic Enrichment
Grade/Age Levels:	Grades 11 and up
Description:	The Carleton Liberal Arts Experience (CLAE) will select 50 high school students who are current sophomores and bring them to Carleton College, all expenses paid, for a one-week summer program. Students of African American descent or students who have an interest in African American culture are encouraged to apply. The CLAE program introduces the strengths of a liberal arts education through an array of courses in science, art, social sciences, and technology. Students should have finished their sophomore year prior to the summer of the program.

MINNESOTA

Program:	Concordia Language Villages
Address:	Concordia College Concordia Language Villages 901 8th St. S Moorhead, MN 56562
Phone:	800-222-4750
Fax:	218-299-3807
E-mail:	clv@cord.edu
Web site:	http://clvweb.cord.edu/prweb
Program Type:	Academic Enrichment
Grade/Age Levels:	Rising grade 9 and up
Description:	Concordia Language Villages offers multiple language programs in Arabic, Chinese, Danish, English, Finnish, French, German, Italian, Japanese, Korean, Norwegian, Portuguese, Russian, Spanish, and Swedish. Students can choose from one-week explorations, 2-week immersions, 4-week for-credit programs, study abroad, and various wilderness/adventure programs.

Program:	**The Institute of Technology Center for Educational Programs (ITCEP)**
Contact:	Enrichment Coordinator
Address:	University of Minnesota The Institute of Technology Center for Educational Programs 4 Vincent Hall 206 Church St. SE Minneapolis, MN 55455
Phone:	612-625-2861
Fax:	612-625-0844
E-mail:	itcep@math.umn.edu
Web site:	http://www.itcep.umn.edu/sumenrich/index.php
Program Type:	Math, Sciences, Engineering, and Computer Science/Technology
Grade/Age Levels:	Grades 3–12
Description:	The Institute of Technology Center for Educational Programs offers summer mathematics enrichment programs for precollege students ages 8–17. Summer enrichment programs for students entering grades 3–12 are held in the Twin Cities at the University of Minnesota. The common purpose of these programs is to keep young students interested in mathematics, science, and engineering, and to give them a realistic picture of what these disciplines are all about. Summer enrichment programs for students entering grades 3–12 are held in the Twin Cities at the University of Minnesota. For high school programs, students must have successfully completed high school level algebra coursework. Students should also possess reasonable maturity and excellent academic skills. For grades 3–9 programs, students participate in day camp activities offered by the University of Minnesota Recreational Sports-Youth Programs Office, and receive 15 hours of math education per week.

MINNESOTA

Program:	**The Works**
Address:	The Works 5701 Normandale Rd. Edina, MN 55424
Phone:	952-848-4848
E-mail:	info@theworks.org
Web site:	http://www.theworks.org/camp.htm
Program Type:	Math, Sciences, Engineering, and Computer Science/Technology; Leadership/Service/Volunteer
Grade/Age Levels:	Ages 5–14
Description:	A "hands-on, minds-on" museum, The Works makes learning about science and technology interesting, understandable, and fun. At The Works, summer campers learn how things work in many areas of science and engineering. Ideal for young men and women who love to explore, discover, design, and build.

Program:	University of Mississippi Summer Accelerated Studies
Address:	Summer Accelerated Studies University of Mississippi Office of Summer School P.O. Box 9 University, MS 38677-0009
Phone:	662-915-1203
Fax:	662-915-1535
E-mail:	umsummer@olemiss.edu
Web site:	http://www.outreach.olemiss.edu/Summer_High_School/accelerated
Program Type:	Academic Enrichment; Math, Sciences, Engineering, and Computer Science/Technology; Leadership/Service/Volunteer
Grade/Age Levels:	Grades 8–12
Description:	Summer Accelerated Studies gives students entering grades 8–10 a taste of college life and possible high school credit. Previous courses offered include geography, environmental science, creative writing, botany, basic computer programming, and a study of Mississippi writers. The program offers both a residential and commuter option.

MISSISSIPPI

Program:	**The University of Southern Mississippi Summer Programs**
Contact:	Dr. Frances Karnes
Address:	The University of Southern Mississippi The Frances A. Karnes Center for Gifted Studies 118 College Dr. #8207 Hattiesburg, MS 39406-0001
Phone:	601-266-5236
Fax:	601-266-4764
E-mail:	gifted.studies@usm.edu
Web site:	http://www.usm.edu/gifted
Program Type:	Leadership/Service/Volunteer; Academic Enrichment
Grade/Age Levels:	Grades 6–11
Description:	The *Leadership Studies Program* is a one-week residential program for students in grades 6–11 who desire to develop and enhance their leadership ability. Leadership I includes the fundamentals necessary for leadership development. Leadership II (prerequisite Leadership I) is a continuation of leadership concepts and qualities. Leadership III (prerequisite Leadership II) focuses on the legal aspects and responsibilities of leadership positions. The *Summer Program for Academically Talented Youth* is a 3-week residential program for students in grades 7–10 who qualify based on SAT or ACT results. A variety of intensive, fast-paced courses are offered, such as precalculus mathematics; human anatomy/physiology; forensic science; polymer science; criminal justice; psychology; creative writing; debate; and political science. The program is designed to include appropriate academic, cultural, and recreational experiences. The University of Southern Mississippi offers the program through cooperative efforts with the Duke University Talent Identification Program.

MISSISSIPPI

Program:	**Cub Creek Science Camp**
Contact:	Ms. Lori Martin, Director
Address:	Cub Creek Science Camp 16795 Highway E Rolla, MO 65401
Phone:	573-458-2125
Fax:	573-458-2126
E-mail:	Director@BearRiverRanch.com
Web site:	http://www.bearriverranch.com
Program Type:	Academic Enrichment
Grade/Age Levels:	Ages 7–16
Description:	A residential summer camp offering one to 6-week sessions, Cub Creek Science Camp offers the ultimate experience for the animal enthusiast. Our camp is home to more than 200 animals from more than 100 different species. We offer one of the only Junior Vet programs in the country. Cub Creek Science Camp combines learning with good old-fashioned fun. Cub Creek is a place where kids can splash in the pool, explore a mud cave, roast marshmallows over a campfire, and make lifelong friends all while learning about science and animals. Campers attend Cub Creek from nearly every state and many other countries.

Program:	**Joseph Baldwin Academy for Eminent Young Scholars**
Address:	Joseph Baldwin Academy for Eminent Young Scholars Truman State University 100 East Normal 203 McClain Hall Kirksville, MO 63501
Phone:	660-785-5406
Fax:	660-785-7460
E-mail:	jmorton@truman.edu
Web site:	http://jba.truman.edu
Program Type:	Academic Enrichment
Grade/Age Levels:	Grades 8–10
Description:	The Joseph Baldwin Academy offers students (rising grades 8–10) the opportunity to engage in an intensive, 3-week residential program with an academically challenging curriculum. Students enroll in one concentrated college course, which meets 6 hours each weekday and 3 hours on Saturdays. Classes are taught by university faculty. The curriculum has included the following courses: Missouri Mammals, Latin, Chemistry, The Horse, An "Animated" Course, Argumentation, The Historian as Programming, Creative Writing, Criminal Justice, Italian Language and Culture, Music, Shakespeare, World Mythology, Language: Myths and Truths, and Native American Frontiers. The Joseph Baldwin Academy is proud to provide an academic challenge to younger students that is truly one of the finest of such opportunities in the nation.

Program:	**Students and Teachers As Research Scientists (STARS)**
Contact:	Dr. Kenneth Mares, Pfizer-Solutia STARS Director
Address:	Students and Teachers As Research Scientists University of Missouri-St. Louis Department of Biology 239 Research Building One University Blvd. St. Louis, MO 63121-4400
Phone:	314-516-6155
Fax:	314-516-6233
E-mail:	diley@umsl.edu
Web site:	http://www.umsl.edu/~sep/stars.htm
Program Type:	Academic Enrichment
Grade/Age Levels:	Grades 11–12
Description:	Fifty high potential, secondary school students (rising juniors and rising seniors) and 10 science teachers have the opportunity to participate in research projects in anthropology, astronomy, biology, chemistry, computer science, earth science, engineering, mathematics, physics, or psychology at one of the collaborating research institutions: Saint Louis University, Washington University, University of Missouri-St. Louis, or Missouri Institute for Mental Health. During this 6-week summer program, students and teachers do research within a community of investigators under the supervision of a practicing research mentor and present their findings in a research paper at the end of the program, which includes an oral presentation of their findings in a seminar format.

Program:	**Montana State University Summer Programs**
Contact:	Ms. Kim Obbink, Director
Address:	Montana State University Office of Continuing Education P.O. Box 172200 Bozeman, MT 59717-2200
Phone:	406-994-6683
Fax:	406-994-6546
E-mail:	ContinuingEd@montana.edu; summer@montana.edu
Web site:	http://www.montana.edu/summer/young.shtml
Program Type:	Academic Enrichment; Fine, Performing, and Visual Arts
Grade/Age Levels:	Grades 2–9
Description:	*Peaks and Potentials* is a residential and commuter camp designed for high-ability and high-potential students. Participants will select from a variety of workshops designed to provide academically challenging opportunities presented by university faculty and other qualified instructors. Recommendation from school personnel is required.
	Museum of the Rockies Children's Summer Camps will offer courses in paleontology, astronomy, geography, space, and Lewis & Clark for children grades 2–5. These will range from day to weeklong experiences. For more information contact Museum of the Rockies at 406-994-6618 or 406-994-5282.
	Summer Youth Orchestra Workshop offers string orchestra lessons and concerts under the guidance of professional musicians. Students study and perform music from various periods at the university and in its surrounding communities. For a brochure or more information contact: Debbie Albin at 406-994-6685.

Program:	**All Girls/All Math Summer Mathematics Camp**
Address:	All Girls/All Math Summer Mathematics Camp University of Nebraska at Lincoln UNL Center for Science, Math, and Computer Education 251 Avery Hall Lincoln, NE 68588-0131
Phone:	402-472-8965
Fax:	402-472-9311
E-mail:	agam@math.unl.edu
Web site:	http://euler.unl.edu/programs/agam
Program Type:	Academic Enrichment
Grade/Age Levels:	Grades 10–12
Description:	All Girls/All Math Summer Camp for high school girls at the University of Nebraska in Lincoln provides a stimulating and supportive environment for girls to develop their mathematical ability and interest. Camp participants take a weeklong course about mathematical codes as well as mini-courses on topics such as bioinformatics, aerodynamics, and knots. The girls will work with female mathematics professors and graduate students, and interact with peers who share an interest in mathematics. Special consideration will be given to those entering their sophomore or junior year and who have successfully completed high school geometry.

NEBRASKA

Program:	**THINK Summer Institute**
Contact:	Ms. Katie Graham, Director of THINK Summer Institute
Address:	Davidson Institute for Talent Development 9665 Gateway Dr., Ste. B Reno, NV 89521
Phone:	775-852-3483 ext. 430
Fax:	775-852-2184
E-mail:	THINK@DITD.ORG
Web site:	http://www.Davidson-Institute.org; http://www.THINKSummerInstitute.org
Program Type:	Academic Enrichment
Grade/Age Levels:	Ages 12–15
Description:	Gifted students interested in a challenging academic summer program should consider attending the THINK Summer Institute on the campus of the University of Nevada, Reno. This intense 3-week residential summer program offers exceptionally gifted 12–15 year-old students the opportunity to earn up to seven transferable college credits.

Program:	**Student Conservation Association**
Contact:	Mr. Douglas Caum, Assistant Director, High School Programs
Address:	Student Conservation Association 689 River Rd. P.O. Box 550 Charleston, NH 03603-0550
Phone:	603-543-1700
Fax:	603-543-1828
E-mail:	realinternships@thesca.org
Web site:	http://www.thesca.org
Program Type:	Internships/Paid Positions
Grade/Age Levels:	Rising grade 10 and up
Description:	With a mission to create the next generation of conservation leaders through active stewardship of the environment, the Student Conservation Association (SCA) is the nation's largest and oldest provider of conservation service opportunities. SCA does this through a tuition-free summer volunteer program for high school students, as well as through a 3–12 month expenses-paid internship program for those 18 and older. Nearly 3,000 SCA members complete more than 1.25 million hours of conservation service annually. Students in grades 10 and up also can take part in the SCA's High School Conservation Crews. Work with natural, cultural resource management agencies (e.g., National Park Service, U.S. Forest Service) and be part of a team of 6–8 students that spends a month on a conservation assignment.

NEW HAMPSHIRE

NEW JERSEY

Program:	**Appel Farm Summer Arts Camp**
Contact:	Ms. Jennie Quinn, Camp Director
Address:	Appel Farm Arts and Music Center 457 Shirley Rd. P.O. Box 888 Elmer, NJ 08318
Phone:	856-358-2472; 800-394-8478
Fax:	856-358-6513
E-mail:	camp@appelfarm.org
Web site:	http://www.appelfarm.org/camp
Program Type:	Fine, Performing, and Visual Arts
Grade/Age Levels:	Ages 9–17
Description:	Appel Farm is a coeducational residential camp with programs in music, theater, dance, visual arts, photography, video, recording arts, creative writing, sports, and swimming. Appel Farm's camp combines arts classes with outdoor activities and community service on its 176-acre property in New Jersey. The student/teacher ratio for courses is 3:1.

Program:	**Coriell Institute for Medical Research Summer Internships**
Contact:	Ms. Charlotte Tule, Director of Human Resources
Address:	Summer Internships Coriell Institute for Medical Research 403 Haddon Ave. Camden, NJ 08103
Phone:	856-966-7377
Fax:	856-964-0254
E-mail:	ctule@coriell.org
Web site:	http://cimr.umdnj.edu
Program Type:	Internships/Paid Positions; Math, Sciences, Engineering, and Computer Science/Technology
Grade/Age Levels:	Grades 12 and up
Description:	College students and high school seniors who are at least 17 years of age and who excel in science are invited to send their resume and cover letter to Coriell Institute for Medical Research, Human Resources Office. Additional information such as his or her accomplishments, interests, and aspirations for the future can be included, as well as a copy of his or her transcript. Internships require a commitment of 8 weeks for high school students. Students work in labs such as the Cryogenics or Tissue Culture laboratory at the Institute and receive a per-hour stipend.

Program:	**Rutgers Young Scholars Program in Discrete Mathematics**
Contact:	Ms. Debbie Toti
Address:	Rutgers Young Scholars Program in Discrete Mathematics Rutgers University SERC Building, Room 225 Busch Campus 118 Frelinghuysen Rd. Piscataway, NJ 08854-8019
Phone:	732-455-2825
Fax:	732-445-3477
E-mail:	toti@dimacs.rutgers.edu
Web site:	http://www.dimacs.rutgers.edu/ysp
Program Type:	Math, Sciences, Engineering, and Computer Science/Technology
Grade/Age Levels:	Grades 9–11
Description:	The Rutgers Young Scholars Program in Discrete Mathematics is designed to encourage talented students, grades 9–11, to consider careers in the mathematical sciences. Selected students participate in an intensive 4-week residential academic program that provides a challenging introduction to discrete mathematics, a new and growing area of the mathematical sciences with many applications on the cutting edge of modern research.

Program:	**American Indian Science and Engineering Society (AISES)**
Address:	American Indian Science and Engineering Society National Headquarters P.O. Box 9828 Albuquerque, NM 87119-9828
Phone:	505-765-1052
Fax:	505-765-5608
E-mail:	info@aises.org
Web site:	http://www.aises.org
Program Type:	Academic Enrichment
Grade/Age Levels:	Grades 9–12
Description:	The American Indian Science & Engineering Society (AISES) is a private, nonprofit organization which nurtures building of community by bridging science and technology with traditional Native values. AISES helps American Indian students prepare for careers in science, technology, engineering, business and other academic areas. American Indians live on lands with abundant natural resources. With proper management of these resources by skilled Indian professionals, tribal nations will be able to diminish the problems that face Indian people and to build strong, sustainable Indian communities. The ultimate goal of AISES is to be a catalyst for the advancement of American Indians as they seek to become self-reliant and self-determined members of society. See Web site for program offerings.

NEW MEXICO

Program:	**University of New Mexico Youth Programs**
Address:	University of New Mexico Continuing Education 1634 University Blvd. NE Albuquerque, NM 87131-4006
Phone:	505-277-0077
Fax:	505-277-1990
E-mail:	registration@dce.unm.edu
Web site:	http://dce.unm.edu/PEP/Youth
Program Type:	Academic Enrichment
Grade/Age Levels:	Ages 5–17
Description:	The University of New Mexico Youth Program has extended course offerings in the summer to get kids and teens involved in learning. Students can select from new courses or strengthen their talent areas. Previous course offerings have included kayaking, drawing and painting, clay sculpting, Spanish, film, rock climbing, and sewing.

Program:	**Academic Study Associates (ASA) Summer Programs in the U. S.**
Contact:	Evan Klavon, Assistant Director
Address:	Academic Study Associates 375 W. Broadway, Ste. 200 New York, NY 10012
Phone:	800-752-2250
Fax:	212-796-8340
E-mail:	Summer@asaprograms.com
Web site:	http://www.asaprograms.com/home/asa_home.asp
Program Type:	Academic Enrichment; Gap Year/Study Abroad/International Travel
Grade/Age Levels:	Grades 9–12
Description:	ASA programs balance expert instruction and scheduled activities with excursions and freedom to foster greater independence and personal growth. In 2007, ASA offered the following programs:

- U.S. Precollege Academic Summer Camp at the University of Massachusetts–Amherst and University of California–Berkeley for grades 9–12;
- College Admissions Prep at Columbia University, Tufts University, and University of California–Berkeley for grades 10–11;

NEW YORK

Program:	**Alfred University Summer Programs for High School Students**
Contact:	Ms. Melody McLay, Director of Summer Programs
Address:	Alfred University Summer Programs for High School Students Carnegie Hall 1 Saxon Dr. Alfred, NY 14802
Phone:	607-871-2612
Fax:	607-871-2045
E-mail:	summerpro@alfred.edu; mclaym@alfred.edu
Web site:	http://www.alfred.edu/summer
Program Type:	Academic Enrichment
Grade/Age Levels:	Grades 10–12
Description:	Alfred University's summer programs invite high school students on campus to learn more about their fields of interest, sample college life, and meet other students with similar interests. The university's programs include:

- *Summer Institutes* in astronomy, creative writing, entrepreneurial leadership, science and engineering, girls' leadership, and portfolio preparation;
- Alfred University's *48-Hour Challenge Science, Math and Engineering Competition* for high school students; and
- *Fast Track Biology I & II*: an intensive summer school course open to high school juniors and seniors.

Program:	**Cooper Union Summer Research Internship Program**
Contact:	Ms. Susan Dorsey, Associate Director
Address:	Summer Research Internship Program The Cooper Union Albert Nerken School of Engineering 51 Astor Pl. New York, NY 10003-7184
Phone:	212-353-4286
Fax:	212-353-4341
E-mail:	dorsey@cooper.edu
Web site:	http://www.cooper.edu/classes/summer/new.html
Program Type:	Math, Sciences, Engineering, and Computer Science/Technology
Grade/Age Levels:	Grades 10–11
Description:	The Summer Research Internship Program provides a great opportunity for high school students to tackle research problems in a college setting. Interns work in teams on applied research projects under the constant guidance of Cooper Union undergraduate teaching assistants. Each project is supervised and mentored by Cooper Union faculty and covers fields such as civil, chemical, electrical, mechanical, biomedical, and environmental engineering, and chemistry.

NEW YORK

Program:	**Cornell Association for the Technological Advancement of Learned Youth in Science and Technology (CATALYST)**
Contact:	Mr. Justin McHorse, Assistant Director of Diversity Programs
Address:	CATALYST–Diversity Programs in Engineering Cornell University College of Engineering 146 Olin Hall Ithaca, NY 14853
Phone:	607-255-0735
Fax:	607-255-2834
E-mail:	jm456@cornell.edu; dlm45@cornell.edu
Web site:	http://www.engineering.cornell.edu/catalyst
Program Type:	Math, Sciences, Engineering, and Computer Science/Technology; Academic Enrichment
Grade/Age Levels:	Grades 10 and up
Description:	The Cornell Association for the Technological Advancement of Learned Youth in Science and Technology (CATALYST) program is a one-week summer residential program for rising high school sophomores, juniors, and seniors from underrepresented backgrounds. CATALYST seeks to advance diversity in engineering and especially encourages members of groups underrepresented in the fields of math, science, and engineering (Blacks, Latino/a, or Native Americans) to apply.

Program:	**Cornell University Summer College Programs for High School Students**
Address:	Cornell University Summer College B20 Day Hall Ithaca, NY 14853-2801
Phone:	607-255-6203
Fax:	607-255-6665
E-mail:	summer_college@cornell.edu
Web site:	http://www.summercollege.cornell.edu
Program Type:	Academic Enrichment
Grade/Age Levels:	Grades 10–12
Description:	Students live on campus for 1, 3, 4, or 6 weeks, take college classes with leading Cornell faculty, earn an average of three to six credits, explore careers and academic majors, enjoy social and cultural activities, and attend admissions workshops. Students may select a program from one or more of the following exploration areas: architecture; art; business; college success; computing and information science; engineering; humanities; law and politics; environmental, agriculture, and applied social sciences; media; medicine, science, and biological research; psychology; veterinary medicine; and writing.

NEW YORK

Program:	**The CURIE Academy**
Contact:	Ms. Sara Hernandez, Assistant Director of Diversity Programs
Address:	The Curie Academy Cornell University College of Engineering 146 Olin Hall Ithaca, NY 14853-2201
Phone:	607-255-0735
Fax:	607-255-2834
E-mail:	sh267@cornell.edu
Web site:	http://www.engineering.cornell.edu/curie
Program Type:	Math, Sciences, Engineering, and Computer Science/Technology; Academic Enrichment
Grade/Age Levels:	Grades 11–12
Description:	The CURIE Academy is a one-week residential program for high school girls who excel in math and science and want to learn more about careers in engineering. CURIE participants take part in classes, lab sessions, and research projects led by Cornell University faculty and graduate students.

Program:	**Environmental Studies Summer Youth Institute (ESSYI)**
Contact:	Professor Jim MaKinster, Director
Address:	Environmental Studies Summer Youth Institute Hobart and William Smith Colleges 300 Pulteney St. Geneva, NY 14456-3397
Phone:	315-781-4400
Fax:	315-781-3000
E-mail:	essyi@hws.edu
Web site:	http://academic.hws.edu/enviro
Program Type:	Academic Enrichment
Grade/Age Levels:	Ages 16–18
Description:	The institute offers a 2-week, college-level interdisciplinary program for talented high school students entering their junior and senior years.

The institute offers a 2-week, college-level interdisciplinary program for talented high school students entering their junior and senior years.

Students will conduct research with Hobart and William Smith faculty members in a variety of locations: On the HWS William F. Scandling (a 65-foot vessel on Seneca Lake), in streams, quaking bogs, the Adirondack Mountains, and the college science laboratories.

Working in the field, in laboratories, in classrooms, and on a 4-day camping trip, students explore a range of topics in environmental policy, economics, and ethics, and come to see the natural world through the eyes of artists, historians, philosophers, and scientists.

NEW YORK

Program:	**Hofstra University Summer Science Research Program (HUSSRP)**
Contact:	Dr. Nanette Wachter, HUSSRP Director
Address:	Hofstra University Summer Science Experiences 151 Hofstra University Chemistry Department Hempstead, NY 11549-1510
Phone:	516-463-5534
Fax:	516-463-6394
E-mail:	chmnwj@hofstra.edu
Web site:	http://www.hofstra.edu/Academics/Colleges/HCLAS/SSE
Program Type:	Math, Sciences, Engineering, and Computer Science/Technology
Grade/Age Levels:	Grades 9–12
Description:	Hofstra University's Summer Science Research Program offers high school students opportunities in science research under the guidance of professionals in science and mathematics. For more than 5 years, HUSSRP has provided selected research-oriented high school students the opportunity to work with our science faculty during the summer in an on-campus research program. The nonresidential 6-week program begins in early July and runs through mid-August culminating in a science "poster session" in September where students display the work they performed during the summer. The poster session is open to all students in the program and gives them the opportunity to present their research to science professionals and their peers in a noncompetitive environment. Students are selected for Hofstra's program on the basis of their high school science experience, research interests, a personal interview, and, above all, a high school teacher's recommendation. Information on additional programs is available on our Web site.

Program:	Link Summer Science Explorations
Address:	Link Summer Science Explorations Kopenik Space Education Center 698 Underwood Rd. Vestal, NY 13850
Phone:	607-748-3685
E-mail:	info@kopernik.org
Web site:	http://www.kopernik.org/summer_science/index.htm
Program Type:	Math, Sciences, Engineering, and Computer Science/Technology
Grade/Age Levels:	Grades 1–12
Description:	The Kopernik Space Education Center in Vestal, NY, is offering weeklong science programs for young people in grades 3–12 as part of our Kopernik Talent Search. We also have an introductory program for students in grades 1 and 2. Sponsored by the Edwin A. and Marion C. Link Foundation in memory of inventor/explorer Ed Link, Link Summer Science Explorations introduces students to hands-on, high-tech science. The Kopernik Link Residential Institutes provide students the opportunity to learn about various aspects of astronomy. Financial assistance is available.

NEW YORK

NEW YORK

Program:	Mecklenburg Conservation Fellowships
Contact:	Dr. Willard Harman, Director
Address:	Mecklenburg Conservation Fellowships State University of New York College at Oneonta Biological Field Station 5838 State Highway 80 Cooperstown, NY 13326-9802
Phone:	607-547-8778
Fax:	607-547-5114
Web site:	http://www.oneonta.edu/academics/biofld/ INTERN/internships.htm
Program Type:	Math, Sciences, Engineering, and Computer Science/Technology
Grade/Age Levels:	Ages 16 and up
Description:	F.H.V. Mecklenburg Conservation Fellowships are awarded to qualified high school students following successful nomination by their teachers, interviews by the Biological Field Station, and consideration of interests, enthusiasm, and academic abilities. The internship lasts 9 weeks and is sponsored by the Biological Field Station. Applicants must be at least 16 years of age. Village of Cooperstown (Susquehanna River) internships also are available to high school students. The purpose of this internship is to monitor water quality in the upper Susquehanna River to assure that the river can safely assimilate effluent from the wastewater treatment facility. This internship is sponsored by the Village of Cooperstown.

Program:	**NSF Plant Genome Research Program**
Contact:	Ms. Elizabeth Fox, Outreach Coordinator
Address:	NSF Plant Genome Research Program Cornell University 217 Boyce Thompson Institute Tower Rd. Ithaca, NY 14853
Phone:	607-254-6732
E-mail:	pgrp-outreach@cornell.edu
Web site:	http://bti.cornell.edu/pgrp
Program Type:	Internships/Paid Positions
Grade/Age Levels:	Grades 9–12
Description:	Summer research internships are available for qualified high school students living within daily driving distance to Cornell University. These internships are full time (40 hours/week) for 6–8 weeks beginning in June. Students will receive a modest stipend, the amount of which will be determined by the lab in which they are placed.

NEW YORK

Program:	**Pace Summer Scholars Program**
Contact:	Ms. Kim Misevis, Program Manager
Address:	Summer Scholars Program Pace University 163 William St., 21st Floor New York, NY 10038
Phone:	212-346-1192
Fax:	212-346-1199
E-mail:	summerscholar@pace.edu
Web site:	http://www.pace.edu/summerscholars
Program Type:	Academic Enrichment
Grade/Age Levels:	Grades 10–11
Description:	Pace University's Summer Scholars Program is open to qualified high school sophomores and juniors who wish to experience college in New York City. They will live in dormitories, attend seminars taught by some of Pace University's best and brightest professors, participate in activities, and meet students who are equally interested in the NYC college experience. Each summer, we offer nine different tracks in which students can major in during the week. Each track contains two courses: one in the morning and one in the afternoon. Upon completion of the program, students will receive a certificate of course completion that will help strengthen college applications.

Program:	**Shoals Marine Laboratory Programs for High School Students**
Address:	Cornell University Shoals Marine Laboratory G-14 Stimson Hall Ithaca, NY 14853-7101
Phone:	607-255-3717
Fax:	607-255-0742
E-mail:	shoals-lab@cornell.edu
Web site:	http://www.sml.cornell.edu/sml_students_highschool.html
Program Type:	Math, Sciences, Engineering, and Computer Science/Technology
Grade/Age Levels:	Grades 11–12
Description:	Shoals Marine Laboratory offers the following summer programs:

- *Marine Environmental Science* focuses on coastal marine habitats, with an emphasis on issues as they relate to global habitats and concerns.
- *Oceanography of the Gulf of Maine* is unique opportunity for students to experience life on board a sailing vessel and on an island off the coast of Maine, studying oceanic and coastal marine environments. The program is located at a marine station in the Gulf of Maine. Students receive three semester credits from Cornell University.

Shoals Marine Laboratory on Appledore Island (summer address):
315 Market St.
Portsmouth, NH 03802

NEW YORK

Program:	**Summer at Rensselaer**
Contact:	Mr. Mike Gunther, Program Manager
Address:	Summer at Rensselaer Rensselaer Polytechnic Institute 110 8th St. Troy, NY 12180
Phone:	518-276-8351
Fax:	518-276-8738
E-mail:	Gunthm@rpi.edu
Web site:	http://summer.rpi.edu
Program Type:	Academic Enrichment
Grade/Age Levels:	Grades K–12
Description:	Rensselaer Polytechnic Institute, a top technological university with an enthusiasm for innovation, offers an exciting summer experience for elementary, middle, or high school students. Summer credit courses are available to academically qualified high school students. Some enrichment programs offered in summer 2007 included: Architecture Career Discovery Program; Computer Game Development Academy; Nature's Treasure Hunt; Robotics Engineering Academy; Young Actors Guild; and Whodunit? The Science of Crime Scenes.

Program:	**Summer in New York: Pre-College Program**
Contact:	Ms. Alexandra Nestoras, Director
Address:	Summer in New York: Pre-College Program
	Barnard College
	Columbia University
	Office of Pre-College Programs
	3009 Broadway (10 Milbank)
	New York, NY 10027-6598
Phone:	212-854-8866
Fax:	212-854-8867
E-mail:	pcp@barnard.edu
Web site:	http://www.barnard.edu/pcp
Program Type:	Academic Enrichment
Grade/Age Levels:	Rising grades 11–12
Description:	The Barnard College Summer in New York City program offers young men and women a unique opportunity to sample precollege courses at one of the nation's premiere colleges, while exploring New York City both in and out of the classroom. Whether you choose our 4-week session, our one-week mini-courses, or our Young Women's Leadership Institute, your studies could include visiting an art gallery, attending a poetry slam or meeting city leaders. Evenings and weekends are packed with organized trips to landmarks like the Statue of Liberty, concerts in Central Park, film festivals, and ethnic neighborhood festivals.

NEW YORK

Program:	**Summer Study Programs**
Contact:	Mr. Bill Cooperman, Executive Director
Address:	900 Walt Whitman Rd. Melville, NY 11747
Phone:	631-424-1000
Fax:	631-424-0567
E-mail:	info@summerstudy.com
Web site:	http://www.summerstudy.com/index.cfm
Program Type:	Academic Enrichment; Math, Sciences, Engineering, and Computer Science/Technology; Leadership/Service/Volunteer
Grade/Age Levels:	Ages 14 and up; Rising grades 10 and up
Description:	*Summer Study at Penn State University* offers both a 6 ½-week and 3 ½-week program in a precollege atmosphere. The longer program allows students to earn college credit by attending freshman-level courses at Penn State. Students live on the Penn State campus. Course listings are available online. *Summer Study at the University of Colorado Boulder* is also a precollege program. Students can choose between the 5-week or 3-week program. The 5-week program allows for college credit courses. The Colorado program includes four great trips: Vail and Breckenridge, Pike's Peak and Colorado Springs, a whitewater rafting adventure, and Rocky Mountain National Park and Estes Park.

Program:	**Telluride Association Summer Programs**
Address:	Telluride Association 217 West Ave. Ithaca, NY 14850
Phone:	607-273-5011
Fax:	607-272-2667
E-mail:	telluride@cornell.edu
Web site:	http://www.tellurideassociation.org
Program Type:	Academic Enrichment
Grade/Age Levels:	Grade 10
Description:	Every summer, the *Telluride Association Sophomore Seminars* (TASS) bring together 54 intellectually motivated high school sophomores for 6-week-long summer programs on the campuses of Indiana University in Bloomington, IN, and the University of Michigan in Ann Arbor, MI. By focusing on intense intellectual exploration within the field of African-American Studies and by selecting many of its students from urban populations underrepresented in similar learning environments, the TASS provides a challenging educational experience that is not easily available to high school students. *Telluride Association Summer Program for Juniors* (TASP) is a 6-week educational experience for high school juniors that offers challenges and rewards rarely encountered in secondary school or even college. Each program is designed to bring together young people from around the world who share a passion for learning. Telluride students, or TASPers, attend a seminar led by college and university faculty members and participate in many other educational and social activities outside the classroom. Every student awarded a place in a TASP attends the program on a full housing, dining, and tuition scholarship. Students pay only the costs of transportation and incidental expenses. Accepted students must provide own transportation to the schools. All other costs are covered by the association.

NEW YORK

Program:	**Union College Summer Programs**
Address:	Union College Office of Special Events 807 Union St. Schenectady, NY 12308
Phone:	518-388-6530
Fax:	518-388-6789
E-mail:	traverc@union.edu
Web site:	http://www.union.edu/summerprograms
Program Type:	Academic Enrichment
Grade/Age Levels:	Rising grades 7–12
Description:	In the *Educating Girls for Engineering* (EDGE) program, 22 high school girls take part in a developmental technologies workshop. In 2007, the workshop was titled "Toys and Tools for Disabled Children." This is a 2-week residential program taught by Union College Faculty.

Five Points is a college-based residential academic program during which students focus on one of eight academic tracks over a 2-week period. Classes include comics and graphic novels, improv comedy, digital creative arts, forensic science, mass media, toy and entertainment engineering, economics, entrepreneurship, and business.

Summer Science Workshop gives economically disadvantaged students the opportunity to attend college-level classes, work in laboratories, and receive career and college guidance for science and health-related fields. This is a 2-week residential program.

Robot Camp introduces middle school and high school students to the exciting world of robots. Students learn to solder and program a bag of parts that will be transformed into working robots. This is a one-week residential program.

Program:	**University of Rochester Summer Programs**
Contact:	Ms. Gayle Jagel, Director
Address:	University of Rochester The Office of Special Programs and Part-time Studies 127 Lattimore Hall Rochester, NY 14627-0358
Phone:	585-275-2344
Fax:	585-461-5901
E-mail:	osp@rochester.edu
Web site:	http://www.rochester.edu/osp
Program Type:	Academic Enrichment
Grade/Age Levels:	Grades 6–12
Description:	The *Rochester Scholars* program provides an exciting academic experience for high school and middle school students to explore the sciences, social sciences, engineering, and humanities in a college campus setting. Students must be currently entering grades 6–12. High school students have the option to enroll in 1, 2, or 3-week sessions over the summer. Middle school students are offered one week of courses during the summer.
	In the *Rochester on Campus* program students entering grades 9–12 have the opportunity to become University of Rochester students for 2, 3, or 4 weeks during the summer. Students get to choose a course of study—for credit (grades 11–12) and non-credit (grades 9–12).
	Taste of College program can help high school students get a jump-start on their college career by allowing rising high school juniors and seniors to take credit classes that are not offered at the high school level or to pursue more rigorous and unique academic challenges. High school juniors and seniors are expected to perform at the college level.

NEW YORK

Program:	**All Arts and Sciences Camp**
Address:	All Arts and Sciences Camp The University of North Carolina at Greensboro Division of Continual Learning 1100 W. Market St. Greensboro, NC 27402-6170
Phone:	336-259-CALL; 866-334-5628
Fax:	336-334-5628
E-mail:	allarts@uncg.edu
Web site:	http://allarts.uncg.edu
Program Type:	Academic Enrichment
Grade/Age Levels:	Ages 7–15
Description:	The All Arts and Sciences camp offers participants ranging from 7 to 15 years old a chance to experience life on a college campus and study various topics in arts and science. Six different campuses in Maryland, Virginia, and North Carolina host these camps. Previous topics studied at the weeklong residential camp have included animation, auto design, fashion design, mathematics and gaming, podcasting, and sports medicine.

Program:	**Davidson July Experience**
Contact:	Ms. Evelyn Gerdes, Director
Address:	Davidson July Experience Davidson College P.O. Box 7151 Davidson, NC 28035
Phone:	704-894-2508
Fax:	704-894-2059
E-mail:	julyexp@davidson.edu
Web site:	http://www.davidson.edu/julyexperience
Program Type:	Academic Enrichment
Grade/Age Levels:	Grades 11–12
Description:	Davidson July Experience is a precollege summer enrichment program for rising high school juniors and seniors. Students enroll in two courses such as Skulls, Bones, and Clandestine Graves; The Art of the Short Story; or The Family and Justice. All courses are taught by a university professor. A limited number of scholarships are available to students with financial need.

NORTH CAROLINA

Program:	Duke University Talent Identification Program (TIP) Summer Programs
Address:	Duke University TIP 1121 W. Main St. Durham, NC 27701-2028
Phone:	919-668-9100
Fax:	919-681-7921
E-mail:	information@tip.duke.edu
Web site:	http://www.tip.duke.edu
Program Type:	Academic Enrichment; Leadership/Service/Volunteer; Gap Year/Study Abroad/International Travel
Grade/Age Levels:	Grade 9–12
Description:	*Duke TIP Domestic Field Studies* allow students in grades 9–12 the opportunity to study creative writing in New Mexico, filmmaking in California, astronomy in North Carolina, and ecology, biology, and geology in Virginia. *Duke TIP Institutes* offer a challenging experience for motivated high school students wishing to gain real-world experience at a top university campus. Great Debates and Leadership Institutes are open to students in grades 9–12 and are held on Duke University's East Campus. The International Affairs Institute is open to students in grades 10–12 and is held on Wake Forest University Campus in Winston-Salem, NC. *Duke TIP International Field Studies* allow students in grades 10–12 the opportunity to study the global economy in China, tropical medicine and tropical ecology in Costa Rica, world politics in England, philosophy and literature in France, and architecture and art history in Italy. *Duke TIP PreCollege Program* provides rising seniors with the opportunity to experience Duke University life before graduating from high school. Participants live on Duke University's West Campus and join undergraduates in their college courses, earning credit and receiving a Duke University transcript. See Web site for details on all of these programs.

Program:	Duke University Youth Programs
Contact:	Mr. Thomas Patterson, Director
Address:	Duke University Youth Programs Duke University Box 90700 Bishop's House Room 201 Durham, NC 27708-0700
Phone:	919-684-6259
Fax:	919-681-8235
E-mail:	youth@duke.edu
Web site:	http://www.learnmore.duke.edu/Youth/programs.htm
Program Type:	Academic Enrichment
Grade/Age Levels:	Rising grades 5 and up
Description:	Several programs, dates vary. Programs have included Action Science Camp, Biosciences and Engineering Camp, Expressions! Performing Arts Camp, Creative Writers' Workshop, Drama Workshop, Young Writers' Camp, and Constructing Your College Experience. Students live on the Duke campus and have the opportunity to participate in additional activities on the weekends. The program offers a limited number of need-based partial scholarships.

NORTH CAROLINA

Program:	**Green River Preserve**
Contact:	Mr. and Mrs. Alexander Schenck, Director
Address:	Green River Preserve 301 Green River Rd. Cedar Mountain, NC 28718
Phone:	828-698-8828
Fax:	828-698-9201
E-mail:	info@greenriverpreserve.org
Web site:	http://www.greenriverpreserve.org
Program Type:	Academic Enrichment; Leadership/Service/Volunteer
Grade/Age Levels:	Ages 9–18
Description:	The Green River Preserve is the setting for our unique natural science oriented summer camp for rising fourth through ninth grade bright young naturalists. We offer 1, 2 and 3-week sessions. These coeducational programs are small by design with a camper to staff ratio of 3 to 1. For rising 9th through 12th graders, we offer Green River Expeditions, a 2-week canoeing, backpacking, and kayaking adventure that follows the Green River tradition of combining learning with exploration. Featured activities include archery, arts and crafts, backpacking, camping skills/outdoor living, canoeing, ceramics/pottery, climbing/rappelling, hiking, and nature/environmental studies.

Program:	**North Carolina School of the Arts Summer Session**
Contact:	Sheeler Lawson, Director of Admissions for Academic Year and Summer Session
Address:	North Carolina School of the Arts Summer Session Office of Admissions 1533 S. Main St. Winston-Salem, NC 27127
Phone:	336-770-3290; 336-770-3264
Fax:	336-770-3370
E-mail:	admissions@ncarts.edu; lawsos@ncarts.edu
Web site:	http://www.ncarts.edu/summersession/index.htm
Program Type:	Fine, Performing, and Visual Arts
Grade/Age Levels:	Grades 9 and up
Description:	The North Carolina School of the Arts 5-week program provides courses in dance, drama, filmmaking, and chamber music. High school and college credit is available. Auditions are required for music and dance. The program also offers shorter programs in fields such as guitar, piano, stage combat, and visual arts. The program offers both residential and commuter options and some financial aid is available.

NORTH CAROLINA

Program:	**North Carolina State University Engineering Summer Programs**
Address:	Engineering Summer Programs North Carolina State University College of Engineering Campus Box 7904 NCSU Raleigh, NC 27695-7904
Phone:	919-515-9669
Fax:	919-515-8702
Web site:	http://www.engr.ncsu.edu/summerprograms
Program Type:	Math, Sciences, Engineering, and Computer Science/Technology
Grade/Age Levels:	Rising grades 11 and 12
Description:	These summer workshops are weeklong residential programs that give students the chance to experience engineering and college life. Classes have included materials science, biological engineering, nuclear engineering, textile engineering, computer science, chemical engineering, motorsports, aerospace engineering, and autonomous robotics. Need-based scholarships available.

Program:	**Space Science Lab Program**
Contact:	Dr. Michael Castelaz, Director, Astronomical Studies and Education
Address:	Space Science Lab Program The Pisgah Astronomical Research Institute 1 PARI Dr. Rosman, NC 28772
Phone:	828-862-5554
Fax:	828-862-5877
E-mail:	mcastelaz@pari.edu
Web site:	http://www.pari.edu/programs/students/ssl
Program Type:	Math, Sciences, Engineering, and Computer Science/Technology
Grade/Age Levels:	Grades 9–12
Description:	The Space Science Lab is a program for high school students to participate in observations of the sun at radio and optical wavelengths. The students begin their observations as resident scientists at PARI during the summer, and then continue their observations remotely during the school year. Space Science Lab students learn and develop skills in electronics, computer sciences, astronomy, physics, and Earth sciences.

NORTH CAROLINA

Program:	**North Dakota Governor's School Programs**
Contact:	Ms. Nancy Suttle, Administrative Officer
Address:	North Dakota Governor's School Programs North Dakota State University Dean's Office, Science and Math Stevens Hall 201 Centennial Blvd. Fargo, ND 58105-5517
Phone:	701-231-7411
Fax:	701-231-7149
E-mail:	nancy.suttle@ndsu.edu; lonnie.hass@ndsu.edu
Web site:	http://www.ndsu.edu/govschool
Program Type:	Math, Sciences, Engineering, and Computer Science/Technology; Fine, Performing, and Visual Arts
Grade/Age Levels:	Grades 11–12
Description:	The North Dakota Governor's School (NDGS) in Science, Mathematics, Business, and Arts is a summer residential program for students who have completed their sophomore or junior year in high school. Governor's School is a 6-week summer program that is held annually on the campus of North Dakota State University in Fargo, ND. Governor's School is funded by the state. Students live in a college dorm, take classes from college professors, and interact with fellow bright individuals in four specialized areas: business, math, science, or the arts. Students attending Governor's School are awarded one high school credit in the discipline they are studying.

OHIO

Program:	**ASM Materials Camp**
Contact:	Ms. Jeane Deatherage, Administrator, Foundation Programs
Address:	ASM Materials Education Foundation 9639 Kinsman Rd. Materials Park, OH 44073-0002
Phone:	440-338-5151; 800-336-5152 (U.S. and Canada)
Fax:	440-338-4634
E-mail:	jeane.deatherage@asminternational.org
Web site:	http://www.asminternational.org/Content/NavigationMenu/ASMFoundation/Materials_Camp/StudentsMaterialsCamp/CampOverview.htm
Program Type:	Math, Sciences, Engineering, and Computer Science/Technology
Grade/Age Levels:	Grades 11–12
Description:	This weeklong academic camp features highly interactive, lab-based activity tailored to the individual interest areas of students entering their junior or senior year in high school. Highly motivated inquisitive learners with math and science aptitude should apply. This camp is free to participants.

Program:	**Case Western Reserve University Precollege Summer Programs**
Address:	Summer Programs Case Western Reserve University 10900 Euclid Ave. Guilford House, Room 412 Cleveland, OH 44106-7158
Phone:	216-368-6735; 216-368-1686
Fax:	216-368-5465
E-mail:	precollege@case.edu
Web site:	http://precollege.case.edu
Program Type:	Academic Enrichment
Grade/Age Levels:	Grades 10 and up
Description:	The Center for Talent Development's summer programs at Case Western Reserve University offer challenging academic classes led by exceptional instructors. Equinox (for students who have completed grades 10–12) and Spectrum (for students who have completed grades 7–9) students will study with knowledgeable instructors in a small, nurturing environment while taking class on a university campus. Both programs encourage critical thinking skills, independent learning strategies, and intellectual self-confidences. Students may select a course in humanities, science, math, or computers and technology. These are joint programs of Northwestern University's Center for Talent Development and Case Western Reserve University.

OHIO

Program:	Kenyon Review Young Writers Summer Program
Contact:	Ms. Anna Duke Reach, Director of Programs
Address:	Kenyon Review Young Writers Summer Program Kenyon College Walton House Gambier, OH 43022-9623
Phone:	740-427-5207
Fax:	740-427-5417
E-mail:	reacha@kenyon.edu; kenyonreview@kenyon.edu
Web site:	http://www.kenyonreview.org/workshops/ywinfo.php
Program Type:	Academic Enrichment
Grade/Age Levels:	Ages 16–18
Description:	The Kenyon Review Young Writers Program is an intensive, 2-week workshop for intellectually curious, motivated high school students (ages 16–18) who value writing. Young Writers takes place at Kenyon College, a leading liberal arts college renowned for its tradition of literary study. The goal of the program is to help students develop their creative and critical abilities with language in order to become more productive writers and more insightful thinkers. Workshop groups (each with 12 students) led by experienced writing instructors, meet for 5 hours a day. In addition to freewriting exercises and responses to prompts, students write stories, poetry, personal narratives, dialogues, reflective passages, and experimental pieces. Participants live in Kenyon College residential halls and have full access to computer labs and recreational facilities. Evening and weekend activities include readings by prominent writers. A teacher's letter of recommendation and a certified high school transcript are due by March 1. Admission is selective and is based primarily on the student's essay and a teacher's recommendation.

Program:	**Miami University Junior Scholars Program**
Contact:	Dr. Robert Smith, Program Director
Address:	Junior Scholars Program Miami University of Ohio 202 Bachelor Hall Oxford, OH 45056-3414
Phone:	513-529-5825
Fax:	513-529-1498
E-mail:	juniorscholars@muohio.edu
Web site:	http://www.muohio.edu/juniorscholars
Program Type:	Academic Enrichment
Grade/Age Levels:	Rising grade 12
Description:	In this precollege program, students earn college credit from a choice of 40 courses. In addition to coursework, scholars attend a series of seminars on topics such as time management and study skills, college admissions, financial aid, interpersonal relationships, cultural awareness, and alcohol awareness. A full schedule of social and recreational activities complements the scholarly parts of the program. Students and staff have the opportunity to participate in swimming, ice-skating, broomball, and volleyball, and they also can enjoy Miami University's Recreational Sports Center. A popular outing every year is the excursion to Kings Island, one of America's best amusement parks.

Program:	**Ross Mathematics Program**
Contact:	Daniel Shapiro, Director
Address:	Ross Mathematics Program The Ohio State University Department of Mathematics 231 W. 18th Ave. Columbus, OH 43210
Phone:	614-292-5101
Fax:	614-292-1479
E-mail:	ross@math.ohio-state.edu
Web site:	http://www.math.ohio-state.edu/ross
Program Type:	Math, Sciences, Engineering, and Computer Science/Technology
Grade/Age Levels:	Ages 14–18
Description:	The Ross Program at the Ohio State University is an intensive summer experience designed to encourage motivated precollege students to explore mathematics. During this 8-week residential program, students are immersed in a world of mathematical discovery. This program is sponsored by the university in partnership with the Clay Mathematics Institute.

Program:	**Wright State University Summer Enrichment Programs**
Contact:	Mr. Chris Hoffman, Assistant Director
Address:	Summer Enrichment Programs Wright State University Office of Pre-College Programs 3640 Colonel Glenn Hwy. Dayton, OH 45435-0001
Phone:	937-775-3135
Fax:	937-775-4883
E-mail:	precollege@wright.edu
Web site:	http://www.wright.edu/academics/precollege
Program Type:	Academic Enrichment
Grade/Age Levels:	Grades 6–12
Description:	The Office of Pre-College Programs offers students entering grades 6–12 the opportunity to attend summer residential enrichment programs. Courses are offered on the following topics: aviation, creative writing, leadership, mathematics, science, television production, theatre, and many more. Each program is comprised of a variety of learning experiences including lectures, hands-on projects, field trips, small group discussions, and learning community activities. Dormitory life, recreation, and social events promote friendships and social interaction among participants. Programs are taught by university faculty, staff, or experts from the local community. Each program has limited enrollment, so register early.

Program:	Oklahoma City University (OCU) Summer Music Programs
Contact:	Ms. JoBeth Moad, Director
Address:	OCU Summer Music Programs Oklahoma City University Performing Arts Academy 2501 N. Blackwelder Oklahoma City, OK 73106
Phone:	405-208-5410
Fax:	405-208-5218
E-mail:	jmoad@okcu.edu
Web site:	http://www.okcu.edu/music/academy
Program Type:	Fine, Performing, and Visual Arts
Grade/Age Levels:	Grades 7–12
Description:	The OCU Summer Music Programs are intensive precollege programs designed for the serious vocalist or instrumentalist. These residential camps offer training in musical theater, voice, opera, strings, brass, percussion, piano, and chamber music. Some scholarships are available.

OKLAHOMA

Program:	**Berry Botanic Garden Apprenticeships in Science and Engineering (ASE)**
Contact:	Kris Freitag, Public Services
Address:	Apprenticeships in Science and Engineering The Berry Botanic Garden 11505 SW Summerville Ave. Portland, OR 97219
Phone:	503-636-4112 ext. 102
Fax:	503-636-7496
E-mail:	register@berrybot.org
Web site:	http://www.berrybot.org/administration/internships.html#high
Program Type:	Internships/Paid Positions
Grade/Age Levels:	Grades 9–12
Description:	The ASE program offers paid internships each summer for students to work with the Berry Botanic Garden's Conservation Program as either a horticulture or conservation intern. Students participate in computer, laboratory, and field research. The Conservation Program works to preserve plant species from both regional and global areas. Projects for 2007 interns included (yet were not limited to) fire restoration research, seed collection and storage, and rare plant reintroduction. See our Web site for details on the internship program activities and application process.

OREGO

SUMMER OPPORTUNITIES FOR TEENS **223**

Program:	**Oregon Museum of Science & Industry Science Camps**
Address:	Oregon Museum of Science & Industry 1945 SW Water Ave. Attn: Camps Portland, OR 97214
Phone:	503-797-4000; 503-797-4662
Fax:	503-797-4568
E-mail:	tneumeyer@omsi.edu; camps@omsi.edu
Web site:	http://www.omsi.edu/camps
Program Type:	Math, Sciences, Engineering, and Computer Science/Technology
Grade/Age Levels:	Ages 7–18
Description:	OMSI combines hands-on science with what kids like best about camp. Campers gain the skills and enthusiasm needed for lifelong learning in a unique setting. This residential camp offers the following activities: aquatic activities, backpacking, camping skills/outdoor living, field trips, hiking, nature/environmental studies, rafting, recreational swimming, team building, wilderness trips, caving, challenge/rope courses, language studies, and snow sports. Visit our Web site for locations.

OREGON

Program:	**Saturday Academy Apprenticeships in Science and Engineering**
Address:	Saturday Academy P.O. Box 8728 Portland, OR 97207
Phone:	503-725-2334; 503-725-2340
Fax:	503-725-2335
E-mail:	ase@saturdayacademy.org
Web site:	http://www.saturdayacademy.org
Program Type:	Math, Sciences, Engineering, and Computer Science/Technology
Grade/Age Levels:	Grades 9–11
Description:	Apprenticeships in Science and Engineering is part of Saturday Academy, a nonprofit organization based in Portland, OR. Students participate in ASE for 8 full-time weeks of work and study with a mentor (at their site) in various fields of science and engineering. Mentors interview and select apprentices in March. Start and end dates are flexible but must occur during the summer school break. Participation in two conferences is mandatory. Housing is the responsibility of apprentices and parents, should the apprentice be selected for a position beyond commuting distance.

Program:	**University of Oregon Summer Enrichment Program**
Contact:	Chris Case, Coordinator
Address:	Summer Enrichment Program University of Oregon 5259 University of Oregon Eugene, OR 97403
Phone:	541-346-1405
Fax:	541-346-3594
E-mail:	sep@oregon.edu; cacase@uoregon.edu
Web site:	http://www.uoyouth.org
Program Type:	Academic Enrichment
Grade/Age Levels:	Grades 6–10
Description:	The University of Oregon offers stimulating academic experiences and spirited social activities in campus-based residential programs for gifted and highly able students currently in grades 6–10. Join us for 2 weeks of learning, laughter, challenges, and fun in a safe and supportive community where intelligence and creativity are valued—where you truly feel like you belong!

OREGON

Program:	**Advanced Writers' Workshops in Fiction, Poetry, and Creative Nonfiction**
Contact:	Dr. Gary Fincke, Director
Address:	Advanced Writers' Workshops in Fiction, Poetry, and Creative Nonfiction Susquehanna University Selinsgrove, PA 17870
Phone:	570-372-4164
Fax:	570-372-2774
E-mail:	gfincke@susqu.edu
Web site:	http://www.susqu.edu/writers/highschoolstudents.htm
Program Type:	Academic Enrichment
Grade/Age Levels:	Grades 11–12
Description:	The Writers' Workshop is open to experienced writers entering 11th or 12th grade. Writers' Workshop attendees are chosen based on teacher/counselor recommendations and portfolio submissions, and each applicant is required to submit 5–6 poems or 6–8 pages of fiction/creative nonfiction.

The week-long experience, now in its 19th summer, provides America's most talented high school writers with the opportunity to work in intensive, small-group workshops headed by nationally recognized authors. The Writers' Workshop features workshops in fiction, creative nonfiction, and poetry.

Program:	**Allegheny College Summer Programs**
Contact:	Ms. Patricia Henry, Director
Address:	Allegheny College Summer Programs Allegheny College 520 N. Main St. Meadville, PA 36335
Phone:	814-332-3100
Fax:	814-332-3101
Web site:	http://www.allegheny.edu/administration/events/summer
Program Type:	Academic Enrichment
Grade/Age Levels:	Ages 3–18
Description:	Allegheny College offers various educational opportunities during the summer months for elementary and high school students. The summer of 2007, for example, included a Theatre Workshop for high school students and camps for children and high school students on topics such as music, dance, and athletics.

Program:	**Carnegie Mellon University Pre-College Programs**
Address:	Carnegie Mellon University Pre-College Programs Office of Admission 5000 Forbes Ave. Pittsburgh, PA 15213-3890
Phone:	412-268-2082
Fax:	412-268-7838
E-mail:	precollege@andrew.cmu.edu
Web site:	http://www.cmu.edu/enrollment/pre-college
Program Type:	Fine, Performing, and Visual Arts; Math, Sciences, Engineering, and Computer Science/Technology
Grade/Age Levels:	Grades 11–12
Description:	• *Advanced Placement Early Action* (APEA) is a challenging credit-bearing program in which students take regular Carnegie Mellon classes for full credit. • The *Architecture Program* is an opportunity for students to explore architecture and to determine their level of interest for further study at the college level. • The *Art Program* is designed as a preparation for applying to and working within a college art program and studio. • The *Design Program* is for students of all skill levels interested in communication or industrial design. • The *Music Program* offers each student the opportunity to follow an individual schedule designed to specific needs and interests, including private study. • The *Drama Program* gives students the chance to participate in a professional training program with three options: acting, musical theater, and design/technical production. • *The National High School Game Academy* (NHSGA) is a 6-week intensive program structured to give students a taste of the current state of video game development and guidance toward embarking on their own career in the video game industry.

Program:	C-MITES Summer Program
Address:	Carnegie Mellon University C-MITES 5136 Margaret Morrison St. MMP30 Pittsburgh, PA 15213-3890
Phone:	412-268-1629
Fax:	412-268-1049
E-mail:	cmites@cmu.edu
Web site:	http://www.cmu.edu/cmites/summer.html
Program Type:	Math, Sciences, Engineering, and Computer Science/Technology
Grade/Age Levels:	Grades 3–8
Description:	One- or 2-week sessions are available throughout the months of June and July. Offered at more than 30 sites throughout Pennsylvania, the Carnegie Mellon Institute for Talented Elementary Students (C-MITES) Summer Program provides students with an opportunity to take a challenging course taught at a fast pace. Interested students may enroll in more than one course. Courses have included aeronautics, architecture, aviation, computer animation, computer programming, forensic science, French, geometry, poetry, TV production, robotics, statistics, Web site design/development, and writing.

PENNSYLVANIA

Program:	**Daniel Fox Youth Scholars Institute**
Contact:	Ms. Cynthia Johnston, Director
Address:	Daniel Fox Youth Scholars Institute Lebanon Valley College of Pennsylvania 101 N. College Ave. Annville, PA 17003
Phone:	717-867-6142; 877-877-0423
E-mail:	johnston@lvc.edu; greenawa@lvc.edu
Web site:	http://www.lvc.edu/ce/youth-scholars/about.aspx
Program Type:	Academic Enrichment
Grade/Age Levels:	Rising grades 10 and up
Description:	The Daniel Fox Youth Scholars Institute is a residential program for exceptional high school students who have completed 9th, 10th, or 11th grade. Students must be nominated for participation in these programs. All admitted students receive full tuition scholarships and need only pay for room and board. Students may choose from 18 different programs. Participants spend a week experiencing life at a college known for its atmosphere of academic excellence and personal attention.

Program:	**Kids College at Penn State Abington**
Address:	Pennsylvania State University Abington Professional Development Office 122 Sutherland Building 1600 Woodland Rd. Abington, PA 19001-3990
Phone:	215-881-7389
Fax:	215-881-7339
E-mail:	jar42@psu.edu
Web site:	http://www.abington.psu.edu/psasite/ce/youthteen/fyf.htm
Program Type:	Academic Enrichment
Grade/Age Levels:	Grades 9–12
Description:	Kids College at Penn State Abington offers a variety of quality learning experiences on a college campus. Students entering grades 9–12 are eligible for the Finding Your Future Program. Some of the topics covered in this program in 2001 included Web graphic design and veterinary medicine. Kids College also offers a variety of camps for all ages, such as science camps, math and physics camps, robotics, computer camps, chess programs, film and TV camps, arts and culture camps, and sports camps.

PENNSYLVANIA

Program:	Leadership, Education, and Development Program in Business, Inc. (L.E.A.D.)
Contact:	Ms. Ayanna Dewer, Program Director
Address:	L.E.A.D. 14 E. Hartwell Lane Philadelphia, PA 19118
Phone:	215-753-2490
Fax:	215-753-2495
E-mail:	info@leadnational.org
Web site:	http://www.leadnational.org/index.html
Program Type:	Academic Enrichment
Grade/Age Levels:	Grade 11
Description:	By encouraging outstanding high school juniors from diverse backgrounds to pursue careers in business, L.E.A.D. is inspiring a new generation of business leaders. Every summer, 12 of the nation's top graduate business schools host an exciting, intensive program where high school juniors are introduced to career opportunities in a variety of disciplines. For 3 to 4 weeks, students live on campus and participate in interactive classes, site visits, and one-on-one sessions conducted by the nation's leading business school professors and corporate executives. Applications must be postmarked by February 1.

PENNSYLVANIA

Program:	The Management & Technology Summer Institute (M&TSI)
Contact:	Ms. Lea Engle, Administrative Director
Address:	The Jerome Fisher Program in Management & Technology The Management & Technology Summer Institute (M&TSI) 3537 Locust Walk, Ste. 100 Philadelphia, PA 19104
Phone:	215-898-7608
Fax:	215-573-7717
E-mail:	mgtech@seas.upenn.edu
Web site:	http://www.upenn.edu/fisher/summer/index.html
Program Type:	Math, Sciences, Engineering, and Computer Science/Technology
Grade/Age Levels:	Grade 12
Description:	M&TSI is a 3-week for-credit summer program for rising high school seniors who want to learn about the integration of technological concepts and management principles. Sponsored by The Jerome Fisher Program in Management and Technology, the School of Engineering and Applied Science, and The Wharton School of the University of Pennsylvania, M&TSI features classes taught by leading faculty and successful entrepreneurs, field trips to companies and research and development facilities, and intensive team projects, as well as other activities designed to give students the opportunity to learn about the principles and practice of technological innovation.

PENNSYLVANIA

Program:	**PECAP Critical and Analytical Reasoning Enrichment (CARE) Program**
Contact:	Dr. Diane Colbert, Director
Address:	Pitt Engineering Career Access Program (PECAP) University of Pittsburgh School of Engineering Ste. B71 Benedum Hall Pittsburgh, PA 15261
Phone:	412-624-0224; 800-296-6856
E-mail:	care@eng.pitt.edu
Web site:	http://www.engr.pitt.edu/diversity/pecap/index.html
Program Type:	Math, Sciences, Engineering, and Computer Science/Technology
Grade/Age Levels:	Rising grades 11–12
Description:	Experience college life in this 5-week residential pre-engineering program at the University of Pittsburgh. CARE emphasizes the development of critical thinking and analytical reasoning skills necessary for careers in science, technology, engineering, and mathematics. Students receive instruction in math and science, SAT preparation, and hands-on projects. Research opportunities are available.

PENNSYLVANIA

Program:	**Pittsburgh Tissue Engineering Initiative (PTEI) Summer Internship Program**
Contact:	Ms. Lashon Jackson, Program Manager
Address:	Summer Internship Program Pittsburgh Tissue Engineering Initiative 100 Technology Dr., Ste. 200 Pittsburgh, PA 15219
Phone:	412-235-5116
Fax:	412-235-5120
E-mail:	ljackson@ptei.org
Web site:	http://www.ptei.org
Program Type:	Internships/Paid Positions; Academic Enrichment; Math, Sciences, Engineering, and Computer Science/Technology
Grade/Age Levels:	Grades 11–12
Description:	The PTEI high school Summer Internship Program was developed with the goal of providing junior and senior high school students with a firsthand opportunity to experience the excitement and vast employment and educational opportunities of careers in science and engineering, as well as to learn more about the field of tissue engineering. The PTEI high school internship will provide opportunities for two or more high school juniors and/or seniors, who will spend 4 weeks learning about tissue engineering research, technologies, and scientific investigations.

High school students may participate in an 8-week Adventures in Biotechnology program, that focuses on the biotech industry.

Middle school students may participate in PTEI summer camp. The 2007 camp, A Starfish Can Grow a New Arm, Why Can't I? was a hands-on experience for students grades 6–8.

Students work in laboratories of scientists at Pittsburgh's leading research centers.

PENNSYLVANIA

Program:	**The University of the Arts Pre-College Summer Institute**
Contact:	Ms. Melissa DiGiacomo, Assistant Director
Address:	Pre-College Summer Institute The University of the Arts 320 S. Broad St. Philadelphia, PA 19102
Phone:	800-616-ARTS
Fax:	215-717-6433
E-mail:	precollege@uarts.edu
Web site:	http://www.uarts.edu/precollege/sum_inst/index.cfm
Program Type:	Fine, Performing, and Visual Arts
Grade/Age Levels:	Grades 10–12
Description:	The 400 students who attend the Pre-College Summer Institute travel to Philadelphia from more than 30 states and numerous nations. They are creative, curious, talented, energetic, and excited about the arts. Our programs foster investigation and exploration of the principles of creativity and focus on the development of each individual student. The Pre-College Summer Institute will challenge your imagination and expose you to dynamic and interesting people, including your peers and your teachers. This is both a residential and commuter program.

Program:	**Digital Video Summer Camp**
Contact:	Tom Dooley, Director
Address:	Digital Video Summer Camp Bryant University Faculty Ste. K 1150 Douglas Pike Smithfield, RI 02917
Phone:	401-232-6422; 800-622-7001
E-mail:	dvcamp@bryant.edu
Web site:	http://www.bryant.edu/dvcamp
Program Type:	Fine, Performing, and Visual Arts
Grade/Age Levels:	Grades 9–12
Description:	Now in its third year at Bryant University's state-of-the art TV studio, Digital Video Summer Camp is for high school students and features two different one-week camps: On-Air Studio Camp and Avid Editing Camp. Each camp gives students a hands-on introduction to the tools and techniques used by film and TV professionals. Register online at our Web site.

RHODE ISLAND

Program:	**Summer Academy in Architecture, Art, and Historic Preservation**
Contact:	Ms. Janet Zwolinski, Assistant Dean
Address:	Summer Academy in Architecture, Art, and Historic Preservation Roger Williams University School of Architecture, Art, and Historic Preservation One Old Ferry Rd. Bristol, RI 02809
Phone:	401-254-3605; 800-458-7144
Fax:	401-254-3565
E-mail:	jzwolinski@rwu.edu
Web site:	http://www.rwu.edu/academics/schools/saahp/lifelonglearning/summeracademy.htm
Program Type:	Academic Enrichment
Grade/Age Levels:	Grade 12
Description:	The Summer Academy in Architecture, Art and Historic Preservation is an intensive 4-week program for high school students who have completed their junior year. The Academy provides a broad and multifaceted framework for students to explore future study and careers in architecture. Areas of study include drawing, architectural design studio, introduction to architecture, and computer applications. The Academy also offers the *Bridge To Success Summer Institute*, which has been in operation since 1999. Our program offers select high school sophomores and juniors the unique opportunity to experience actual college life, while at the same time preparing them for the challenging SAT exam.

Program:	Carolina Journalism Institute
Contact:	Ms. Karen Flowers
Address:	Carolina Journalism Institute University of South Carolina School of Journalism and Mass Communications Columbia, SC 29208
Phone:	803-777-6284
Fax:	803-777-4103
E-mail:	schopress@gwm.sc.edu; flowersk@gwm.sc.edu
Web site:	http://www.sc.edu/cmcis/so/cji/index.html
Program Type:	Academic Enrichment
Grade/Age Levels:	Grades 6–12
Description:	This intensive 5-day regional workshop helps middle and high school students and advisers sharpen their skills in publication, production, interviewing, writing, editing, design, and leadership for broadcast, literary magazines, newspapers, and yearbooks. Participants will attend large group sessions and individual classes that focus on broadcast, business, desktop publishing, journalistic writing, literary magazine, newspaper, photojournalism, and yearbook. Both beginning and advanced classes will be offered.

Program:	**Summer Scholars Program at Furman University**
Contact:	Jean M. Adams, Director
Address:	Summer Scholars Program Furman University 3300 Poinsett Highway Greenville, SC 29613
Phone:	864-294-3231
Fax:	864-294-2018
E-mail:	jean.adams@furman.edu
Web site:	http://www.furman.edu/summerscholars
Program Type:	Academic Enrichment
Grade/Age Levels:	Grades 11–12
Description:	Furman University's Summer Scholars Programs are one-week academic enrichment programs designed for rising juniors and seniors in high school (rising sophomores may be considered for certain programs). Students study under the direction of Furman faculty members in small group settings. Summer Scholars programs typically include a variety of learning experiences such as lectures, class discussions, debates, laboratory experiences, field trips, group and individual projects, and other activities intended to provide an enjoyable and challenging learning experience for participants.

Program:	**University of South Carolina Summer Conservatories**
Contact:	Ms. Marissa Freeman, Program Coordinator
Address:	University of South Carolina 1300 Wheat St. Columbia, SC 29208
Phone:	803-777-7264
Fax:	803-777-6250
E-mail:	freemanM@gwm.sc.edu; susanea@gwm.sc.edu
Web site:	http://www.cas.sc.edu/dance/Dance/entrance.html; http://www.music.sc.edu/EventsWorkshops/cmf
Program Type:	Fine, Performing, and Visual Arts
Grade/Age Levels:	Ages 11 and up
Description:	• The South Carolina *Summer Dance Conservatory* is a 3-week residential youth program offering intensive training in classical ballet or jazz. Acceptance is by audition for ages 11 years and older. Videotape (VHS) auditions are permitted. Call for audition sites and times. • The South Carolina *Summer Music Conservatory* is an intensive one-week training period focusing on individual performance and chamber music.

Program:	**South Dakota Ambassadors of Excellence Program**
Contact:	Dr. Tim Duggan, Director or Heath Weber, Ambassadors Director
Address:	South Dakota Ambassadors of Excellence Program The University of South Dakota Division of Curriculum and Instruction School of Education 414 E. Clark St. Vermillion, SD 57069
Phone:	605-677-5832; 605-677-5210
Fax:	605-677-3102
E-mail:	timothy.duggan@usd.edu
Web site:	http://www.usd.edu/ed/ci/gifted/ambassadors.cfm
Program Type:	Leadership/Service/Volunteer
Grade/Age Levels:	Grades 10–12
Description:	This summer program is designed for selected former South Dakota Governor's Camp participants and other students of high ability in rising grades 10–12. The mission is to provide an optimum learning experience for South Dakota's gifted high school students in a safe and supportive environment, emphasizing service, leadership, and artistic potential. The program includes team-building activities, educational exploratory sessions, a community service project, and more.

Program:	**South Dakota Governor's Camp**
Contact:	Dr. Tim Duggan, Director
Address:	South Dakota Governor's Camp The University of South Dakota Division of Curriculum and Instruction School of Education 414 E. Clark St. Vermillion, SD 57069
Phone:	605-677-5832
Fax:	605-677-3102
E-mail:	Timothy.Duggan@usd.edu
Web site:	http://www.usd.edu/ed/ci/gifted/governorscamp.cfm
Program Type:	Academic Enrichment
Grade/Age Levels:	Grades 7–9
Description:	The mission of the South Dakota Governor's Camp is to provide an optimum learning experience for bright children in a safe and supportive environment. The Governor's Camp provides academic enrichment experiences with USD faculty and trained staff. Students participate in recreational programs using campus facilities and have a full schedule of challenging activities with other bright students.

SOUTH DAKOTA

TENNESSEE

Program:	The Girls and Science (GAS) Camp
Contact:	Mr. Joe Lopez, Program Coordinator
Address:	The Girls and Science (GAS) Camp Vanderbilt Center for Science Outreach 806 Light Hall Nashville, TN 37232-0670
Phone:	615-332-7140
Fax:	615-332-7140
E-mail:	cso@vanderbilt.edu
Web site:	http://www.girlsandscience.org
Program Type:	Math, Sciences, Engineering, and Computer Science/Technology
Grade/Age Levels:	Rising grades 7–9
Description:	The Girls and Science (GAS) Camp was established at Vanderbilt University in the summer of 1999 in response to the gender differences found in high school science achievement. The goals of the GAS Camp are to engage girls in science activities, to foster confidence in science achievement, and to encourage girls' enrollment in high school science courses. During the summer, two weeklong day sessions are held for current seventh graders and two are held for current eighth graders. The camp is held in the biosciences laboratories at Vanderbilt and staffed by local science teachers and science education students from Vanderbilt. Activities address a variety of scientific fields and are appropriate for any girl who is interested in science.

Program:	**Vanderbilt University PAVE**
Contact:	Dr. John Veillette, Associate Dean and Director of PAVE
Address:	Vanderbilt University PAVE VU Station B 351736 Nashville, TN 37235-1736
Phone:	615-322-7827
Fax:	615-322-3297
E-mail:	pave@vanderbilt.edu
Web site:	https://pave.vanderbilt.edu/ayindex.php
Program Type:	Math, Sciences, Engineering, and Computer Science/Technology
Grade/Age Levels:	Grades 11–12
Description:	PAVE is a 6-week summer course of study designed to strengthen the academic skills of students who are planning to enter a college engineering, premedical, science, or technology program. The program introduces students to college life while improving their problem-solving, technical writing, computer, and laboratory skills.

TENNESSEE

Program:	**Aquatic Sciences Adventure Camp**
Contact:	Lendon Gilpin, Assistant Director for Education
Address:	Aquatic Sciences Adventure Camp Texas State University Edwards Aquifer Research and Data Center 248 Freeman Bldg. San Marcos, TX 78666-4616
Phone:	512-245-2329
Fax:	512-245-2669
E-mail:	LG16@txstate.edu
Web site:	http://www.eardc.txstate.edu/camp.html
Program Type:	Academic Enrichment
Grade/Age Levels:	Ages 9–15
Description:	Aquatic Sciences Adventure Camp is a fun camp for students who are interested in aquatic or marine sciences. The program includes a mixture of educational and recreational activities, including aquatic biology and water chemistry, swimming, tubing, scuba/snorkeling, river rafting, a glass-bottom boat ride, a Sea World trip, and more. The residential coeducational camp is conducted during weekly sessions in June and July.

TEXAS

Program:	AwesomeMath Summer Program
Contact:	Dr. Titu Andreescu
Address:	AwesomeMath Summer Program University of Texas at Dallas School of Natural Sciences and Mathematics Mail Station FN 33 2601 N. Floyd Rd. Richardson, TX 75083
Phone:	214-549-6146
Fax:	972-542-8039
E-mail:	info@awesomemath.org; titu@awesomemath.org
Web site:	http://www.awesomemath.org/summer.shtml
Program Type:	Math, Sciences, Engineering, and Computer Science/Technology
Grade/Age Levels:	Grades 7–11
Description:	The AwesomeMath Summer Program is a 3-week residential camp designed to hone middle school and high school students' mathematical problem-solving skills up to the Olympiad level. Each student takes two courses of his or her choice meant to increase problem-solving skills. Recreational activities are also provided.

TEXAS

Program:	**Camp on the Coast Summer Theatre Workshop**
Contact:	Mr. Kelly Russell
Address:	Camp on the Coast Texas A&M University at Corpus Christi 6300 Ocean Dr., Unit 5722 Corpus Christi, TX 78412
Phone:	361-825-5777; 361-825-2250
Fax:	361-825-2778
E-mail:	Kelly.Russell@tamucc.edu
Web site:	http://theatre.tamucc.edu/camp07.htm
Program Type:	Fine, Performing, and Visual Arts
Grade/Age Levels:	Grades 9–12
Description:	The Texas A&M University at Corpus Christi Summer Theatre Workshop is a 2-week residential camp designed for high school students seeking a highly intensive and creative theatre experience. Participants will rehearse and perform in a one-act play directed by one of four highly successful theatre educators. Students will also study acting, voice, and movement in morning classes taught by TAMU-CC Theatre faculty.

TEXAS

Program:	**CATS Summerstars Comprehensive Musical Theatre Workshop**
Address:	Summerstars Comprehensive Musical Theatre Workshop Creative Arts Theatre and School 1100 W. Randol Mill Rd. Arlington, TX 76012
Phone:	817-861-2287; 817-265-8512
Fax:	817-274-0793
Web site:	http://www.creativearts.org/summerstars.html
Program Type:	Fine, Performing, and Visual Arts
Grade/Age Levels:	Rising grades 7–12
Description:	Creative Arts Theater and School (CATS) Summerstars Workshop is a 2-week comprehensive residential and commuter program for gifted and talented students taught by professional actors, directors, choreographers, and musicians. The program concludes with a full musical production for family and friends of participants on the final Saturday. See Web site for 2008's camp production information.

TEXAS

Program:	**Clark Scholars Program at Texas Tech University**
Contact:	Dr. Michael San Francisco, Director
Address:	Clark Scholars Program Texas Tech University Box 43131 Lubbock, TX 79409-3131
Phone:	806-742-2706
Fax:	806-742-2963
E-mail:	michael.sanfrancisco@ttu.edu
Web site:	http://www.clarkscholars.ttu.edu
Program Type:	Academic Enrichment
Grade/Age Levels:	Rising grades 11 and up
Description:	The Clark Scholar Program is an intensive 7-week summer research program for highly qualified high school juniors and seniors. The scholars will receive a $750 tax-free stipend and room and board. Students work with university faculty in research areas including animal science, civil engineering, classical languages, nutrition, philosophy, and wildlife management.

TEXAS

Program:	**Gifted Students Institute College Experience**
Contact:	Ms. Marilyn Swanson, Director of Programming
Address:	Southern Methodist University Gifted Students Institute College Experience P.O. Box 750383 Dallas, TX 75275-0383
Phone:	214-768-0123
Fax:	214-768-3147
E-mail:	gifted@smu.edu
Web site:	http://www.smu.edu/ce
Program Type:	Academic Enrichment
Grade/Age Levels:	Grades 11–12
Description:	Academically talented high school students can get a head start on college and a taste of campus life during this exciting 5-week summer program at SMU. The selection of college-credit subjects for morning classes includes philosophy, English, math, psychology, history, and government. In the afternoon, all College Experience students will participate in a "core" class or humanities overview class for three hours of college credit. Students who elect to live in the CE residence hall will participate in special cultural, educational, and recreational activities.

TEXAS

Program:	**Gifted Students Institute Talented and Gifted Program**
Contact:	Ms. Marilyn Swanson, Director of Programming
Address:	Southern Methodist University Gifted Students Institute Talented and Gifted Program P.O. Box 750383 Dallas, TX 75275-0383
Phone:	214-768-0123
Fax:	214-768-3147
E-mail:	gifted@smu.edu
Web site:	http://www.smu.edu/tag
Program Type:	Academic Enrichment
Grade/Age Levels:	Rising grades 8–10
Description:	During this 3-week residential program, students participate in two stimulating classes chosen from a wide selection of SMU credit and noncredit courses. Cultural enrichment activities are provided for all TAG students. Three-hour credit courses include leadership, mathematical sciences, political science, mechanical engineering, psychology, philosophy, and ethics. Noncredit courses include writing, engineering, theater arts, public discourse, mathematics, music, photography, physics, geography, and rocketry. Enrollment is limited to 80 students. Participants are selected on the basis of academic ability and motivation as demonstrated by grades, SAT or ACT scores, teacher recommendations, and other application requirements.

TEXAS

Program:	**High School Summer Science Research Program (HSSSRP)**
Contact:	Ms. Suzanne Keener, Administrative Associate or Dr. Frank Mathis, Director
Address:	High School Summer Science Research Fellowship Program Baylor University One Bear Place #97344 Waco, TX 76798
Phone:	254-710-4288
Fax:	254-710-3639
E-mail:	HSSSRP@baylor.edu
Web site:	http://www.baylor.edu/summerscience
Program Type:	Math, Sciences, Engineering, and Computer Science/Technology
Grade/Age Levels:	Rising grade 12
Description:	The purpose of the High School Summer Science Research Program (HSSSRP), an annual program established in 1991, is to give superior high school students hands-on research experience by working on research projects with Baylor University science professors in many disciplines. The fellowship program occurs during the University's first session of summer school and is open to students between their junior and senior year of high school. The residential program lasts 5 weeks. Ten students are selected each year from high schools throughout the U.S. to be involved with this program. Students completing the program earn one semester hour of college credit.

TEXAS

Program:	**Institute for the Development and Enrichment of Advanced Learners (IDEAL) at Texas Tech University**
Contact:	Ms. Martha Hise, Director
Address:	Institute for the Development and Enrichment of Advanced Learners Texas Tech University Box 41008 Lubbock, TX 79409-1008
Phone:	806-742-2420
Fax:	806-742-0480
E-mail:	m.hise@ttu.edu
Web site:	http://www.ideal.ode.ttu.edu
Program Type:	Academic Enrichment; Math, Sciences, Engineering, and Computer Science/Technology; Fine, Performing, and Visual Arts; Leadership/Service/Volunteer
Grade/Age Levels:	Grades K–12
Description:	IDEAL offers distinctive academic enrichment programs to high-achieving children in grades K–12 to promote academic excellence, citizenship, leadership, diversity, and appreciation of the arts. Programs include Super Saturdays, Shake Hands With Your Future, and Science: It's a Girl Thing.

Program:	**Lone Star Leadership Academy**
Contact:	Ms. Monica Hayes, Educational Outreach Director
Address:	Education in Action P.O. Box 1171 Hurst, TX 76053
Phone:	817-285-8961
Fax:	817-285-8874
E-mail:	admissions@educationinaction.org
Web site:	http://www.educationinaction.org
Program Type:	Leadership/Service/Volunteer
Grade/Age Levels:	Grades 5–8
Description:	Participants travel to Dallas/Fort Worth, Austin, and Houston/Galveston to experience curriculum taught in Texas classrooms through historically, politically, scientifically, and environmentally significant sites. Career speakers introduce participants to a wide variety of career and internship opportunities. Texas teachers facilitate leadership groups, simulations, and leadership activities.

TEXAS

Program:	**Longhorn Music Camp**
Address:	Longhorn Music Camp University of Texas at Austin 1 University Station E3100 Austin, TX 78712
Phone:	512-232-2080
Fax:	512-232-3907
E-mail:	lmc@www.utexas.edu
Web site:	http://www.longhornmusiccamp.org
Program Type:	Fine, Performing, and Visual Arts
Grade/Age Levels:	Grades 6–11
Description:	Longhorn Music Camp provides summer music programs for students completing grades 6–11 in band, orchestra, choir, harp, and piano (disciplines vary by grade). This program includes both residential and commuter options. Some of the programs require auditions.

Program:	**Science, Technology & Robotics Camp**
Contact:	Mr. Jim McMillan, Director
Address:	Science, Technology & Robotics Camp 728 Evergreen Hills Rd. Dallas, TX 75208
Phone:	214-521-1444
E-mail:	mcmillan01@flash.net
Web site:	http://www.kinetic-learning-center.com/camp2.ivnu
Program Type:	Math, Sciences, Engineering, and Computer Science/Technology
Grade/Age Levels:	Ages 7–18
Description:	This camp teaches students the basics of electronic arts, including soldering, kit building, robotics, and how to build remote-controlled objects. The camp fills quickly. See session descriptions online for specific age requirements.

Program:	Sea Camp and SeaWorld
Contact:	Ms. Daisy Puccetti, Interim Director
Address:	Sea Camp and SeaWorld Texas A&M at Galveston P.O. Box 1675 Galveston TX 77553
Phone:	409-740-4525; 1-87-SEA-AGGIE
Fax:	409-740-4894
E-mail:	seacamp@tamug.edu
Web site:	http://www.tamug.edu/seacamp; http://www.seaworld.org/adventure-camps/swt/resident/index.htm
Program Type:	Math, Sciences, Engineering, and Computer Science/Technology
Grade/Age Levels:	Ages 10–18
Description:	Texas A&M University at Galveston offers educational outreach programs to people of all ages. *Sea Camp* is a weeklong residential adventure exploring the wonders of the marine and estuarine environments for campers ages 10–18. As a Sea Camper you will have access to research vessels, oceanographic equipment, laboratory facilities, and a professional staff enabling you to learn about the ocean through hands-on experiences. Each *SeaWorld/Busch Gardens* resident camp session gives you up-close, behind-the-scenes, hands-on experiences with amazing animals, including many that are threatened or endangered. Alongside veterinarians, trainers and other animal care experts, you'll have the opportunity to feed, interact with and care for animals ranging from belugas and manatees, to giraffes and great apes. Swim with dolphins, snorkel, kayak, surf, and much more.

Program:	**Summer Academy in Architecture**
Address:	Summer Academy in Architecture The University of Texas at Austin 1 University Station–B7500 Austin, TX 78712-0222
Phone:	512-471-9890
Fax:	512-471-7033
E-mail:	caad@lists.cc.utexas.edu
Web site:	http://www.utexas.edu/architecture/center/academy
Program Type:	Academic Enrichment; Fine, Performing, and Visual Arts
Grade/Age Levels:	Ages 16 and up
Description:	The Center for American Architecture and Design coordinates and hosts the School of Architecture's Summer Academy in Architecture program. The Summer Academy is an introductory course in architecture that assumes no prior study in the field, but rather a great familiarity with it through the experience of occupying places. The 5-week session focuses on a series of individual design projects that introduce many of the important aspects of the field and encourage a personal exploration into architecture's inherent interests.

TEXAS

Program:	**Summer Creative Writing Workshops**
Contact:	Mr. Jack McBride, Program Coordinator
Address:	Summer Creative Writing Workshops Rice University School Literacy and Culture Project Writers in the Schools 1523 W. Main Houston, TX 77006
Phone:	713-523-3877
Fax:	866-793-4865 (toll-free)
E-mail:	mail@witshouston.org
Web site:	http://www.witshouston.org
Program Type:	Academic Enrichment
Grade/Age Levels:	Grades Pre-K–12
Description:	The Summer Creative Writing Workshops offer a supportive environment where children engage in writing stories, poetry, essays, and plays to discover the joys of writing. These 3-week camps are taught by professional writers and local teachers.

Program:	**Summer Strings Music Camp**
Contact:	Mr. Royce Coatney
Address:	Summer Strings Music Camp University of Texas at Arlington Box 19105 Arlington, TX 76019
Phone:	817-272-3471; 817-469-1393
Fax:	817-272-3434
E-mail:	roycecoatney@sbcglobal.net
Web site:	http://www.uta.edu/music/summercamps/strings/index.html
Program Type:	Fine, Performing, and Visual Arts
Grade/Age Levels:	Grades 6–12
Description:	This annual program provides young string players an opportunity to improve their musical skills and develop new friendships with students from around the state. Students participate in daily rehearsals, sectionals, and classes in music theory, music history, and conducting. All State Masterclasses are available for high school students. All students audition for placement in one of six orchestras.

TEXAS

Program:	**Texas A&M University at Galveston TAG**
Contact:	Ms. Daisy Puccetti, Interim Director
Address:	Texas A&M University at Galveston TAG P.O. Box 1675 Galveston, TX 77553
Phone:	409-740-4525
Fax:	409-470-4894
E-mail:	duersond@tamug.edu
Web site:	http://www.tamug.edu/seacamp/newweb/TAG.html
Program Type:	Math, Sciences, Engineering, and Computer Science/Technology
Grade/Age Levels:	Grades 8–12
Description:	TAG, a residential summer program for high ability students in grades 8–12, is being offered this summer at Texas A&M University at Galveston. These career-oriented courses will help students expand their horizons with a preparatory course in the field of their choice: veterinary medicine, marine engineering, premedicine, or marine biology research.

Program:	Texas Brigades Wildlife Education and Leadership Development Camps
Contact:	Ms. Helen Holdsworth, Executive Director
Address:	Wildlife Education and Leadership Development Camps Texas Brigades 2800 NE Loop 410, Ste. 105 San Antonio, TX 78218
Phone:	210-826-2904; 800-TEX-WILD
Fax:	210-826-4933
E-mail:	h_holdsworth@texas-wildlife.org
Web site:	http://www.texasbrigades.org
Program Type:	Leadership/Service/Volunteer
Grade/Age Levels:	Ages 13–17
Description:	The Texas Brigades is a wildlife-focused program for high school students. Our mission is to empower high school youth with the necessary skills and knowledge in wildlife and fisheries, habitat conservation, land and water stewardship, team-building, communication, and leadership to become ambassadors for conservation in order to ensure a sustained wildlife and fisheries legacy for future generations. There are four different camps: Bobwhite Brigade, Buckskin Brigade, Feathered Forces, and Bass Brigade. Each 4½-day camp is instructed by top wildlife professionals and resource managers.

TEXAS

Program:	**Texas Honors Leadership Program**
Contact:	Dr. Dorothy Sisk
Address:	Texas Honors Leadership Program Lamar University P.O. Box 10034 Beaumont, TX 77710
Phone:	409-880-8046
Fax:	409-880-8384
E-mail:	siskda@my.lamar.edu
Web site:	http://dept.lamar.edu/connchair/THLP/Main.htm
Program Type:	Academic Enrichment
Grade/Age Levels:	Grades 11 and up
Description:	The Texas Honors Leadership Program is a summer residential program at Lamar University in Beaumont, TX, that provides innovative academics for gifted adolescents (finishing their sophomore year). The 3-week program offers courses not usually provided in high school that emphasize hands-on activities designed to help students develop their leadership and ethical decision-making skills. Students actively participate in cognitively challenging tasks that build on their ability to think, reflect, and experience success. Evening seminars are provided with individuals who have demonstrated leadership at the state, national, and international levels. Students host these sessions and engage in lively Q&A with eminent leaders in business, sciences, and the arts.

TEXAS

Program:	**Texas State University Honors Summer Math Camp**
Contact:	Dr. Max Warshauer, Director
Address:	Texas State University Honors Summer Math Camp Texas Mathworks 601 University Dr. San Marcos TX 78666
Phone:	512-245-3439
Fax:	512-245-1469
E-mail:	mathworks@txstate.edu; max@txstate.edu
Web site:	http://www.txstate.edu/mathworks/camps/hsmc.html
Program Type:	Academic Enrichment; Math, Sciences, Engineering, and Computer Science/Technology
Grade/Age Levels:	Grades 10–12
Description:	The goal of the Texas State Honors Summer Math Camp is to excite talented young students about doing mathematics, to teach students to reason rigorously and precisely, and to develop questioning minds. The focus on number theory is modeled after the Ross Summer Program at Ohio State, teaching students to "think deeply of simple things" (Arnold Ross). Students work together exploring ideas and share in the excitement of finding the simple mathematical ideas that underline and explain seemingly complex problems. First-year students take courses in elementary number theory, mathematical computer programming, and an honors seminar. Returning students study combinatorics, analysis, and selected short courses. Advanced students may also work on a supervised Siemens Competition research project.

TEXAS

Program:	**Texas State University Junior Summer Math Camp**
Contact:	Mr. Max Warshaver, Director
Address:	Texas State University Junior Summer Math Camp 601 University Dr. San Marcos, TX 78666
Phone:	512-245-3439
Fax:	512-245-1469
E-mail:	mathworks@txstate.edu
Web site:	http://www.txstate.edu/mathworks/camps/jsmc.html
Program Type:	Math, Sciences, Engineering, and Computer Science/Technology; Academic Enrichment
Grade/Age Levels:	Rising grades 4–8
Description:	The Texas State Junior Summer Math Camp is a nationally recognized math program for students in grades 4–8. There are five levels in the program. Level 1, the Mathematical Mystery Tour, is for students in grades 4–5. It introduces students to the basic ideas in algebra through the use of children's drama and activities. Level 2, MathQuest, is for students in grades 5–6, and it introduces students to functions, fractions, decimals, and using a graphing calculator. Level 3, Math Explorations, is for students in grades 6–7. This level introduces algebraic concepts motivated by geometry. Levels 1–3 prepare students to study algebra, while introducing students to the excitement of doing math together. In Level 4, Combinatorics, students study basic counting principals and discrete math, which are topics often overlooked in the standard school curriculum. Level 5 includes a special residential training program for top students throughout Texas.

TEXAS

Program:	University for Young People
Contact:	Dr. Mary M. Witte, Director
Address:	University for Young People Baylor University Center for Community Learning and Enrichment One Bear Place #97282 Waco, TX 76798
Phone:	254-710-2171; 800-BAYLOR-U
Fax:	254-710-4909
E-mail:	K-12andProfDev@baylor.edu
Web site:	http://www.baylor.edu/SOE/CCLE
Program Type:	Academic Enrichment
Grade/Age Levels:	Grades 1–12
Description:	University for Young People is a summer enrichment program for rising first graders through rising twelfth graders. Younger students meet at an elementary school to study an interdisciplinary theme such as Structures where they discover the many structures that are involved in building a new city. Older students attend classes on the Baylor campus in the sciences, social sciences, fine arts, and technology.

TEXAS

Program:	**Upward Bound Math and Science Program**
Address:	Upward Bound Math and Science Program University of Texas at Arlington Box 19356 706 Carlisle Hall Arlington, TX 76019
Phone:	817-272-2636
Fax:	817-272-2616
E-mail:	ubms@uta.edu
Web site:	http://www.uta.edu/upward; http://www.uta.edu/ubmathsci
Program Type:	Math, Sciences, Engineering, and Computer Science/Technology
Grade/Age Levels:	Grades 9–11
Description:	The University of Texas at Arlington Upward Bound Math and Science Regional Center is a concentrated program open to those students who have demonstrated potential in the fields of mathematics, science and/or engineering. Annually, students are selected from the states of Arkansas, Louisiana, New Mexico, Oklahoma, and Texas to attend this school. The Upward Bound Program Summer Component is an extension of the academic year and offers participants the opportunity to further receive academic enrichment in preparation for the upcoming school year, as well as get a glimpse of what college life is like. Participants live and study on the UT Arlington campus for 6 weeks beginning in June.

Program:	**USA Chess National Summer Chess Camp Tour**
Contact:	Mr. Mike Borchelt
Address:	USA Chess National Summer Chess Camp Tour 18911 Forest Bend Creek Way Spring, TX 77379
E-mail:	mborchelt@usachess.com
Web site:	http://www.chesscamp.com
Program Type:	Academic Enrichment
Grade/Age Levels:	Ages 5–16
Description:	USA Chess provides chess activities for children in more than 80 US cities. Activities include a national summer chess camp tour, scholastic tournaments, school chess programs, and private/group lessons. Camps take place in Houston and Dallas, TX, Cape Cod, MA, and Honolulu, HI.

TEXAS

Program:	WE CAN: Women in Engineering: Curriculum, Applications, and Networking
Contact:	Dr. Tanja Karp
Address:	WE CAN: Women in Engineering: Curriculum, Applications, and Networking Texas Tech University Electrical and Computer Engineering P.O. Box 43102 Lubbock, TX 79409-3102
Phone:	806-742-0140
E-mail:	Tanja.Karp@ttu.edu
Web site:	http://www.ee.ttu.edu/ece2/wecan/wecan.html
Program Type:	Math, Sciences, Engineering, and Computer Science/Technology
Grade/Age Levels:	Grade 11
Description:	The goal of the WE CAN summer camp is to provide a stimulating and confidence building environment to young women who are academically qualified to pursue careers in engineering, specifically in electrical and computer engineering. The program curriculum is project oriented, with students completing a number of software and hardware based projects during the 2-week camp. Teamwork and collaboration will be emphasized. Sessions will focus on different areas within electrical and computer engineering, giving participants a good overview of what electrical and computer engineers do and what the electrical and computer engineering curriculum is like. Students accepted to the program must be female high school juniors and be currently enrolled in precalculus or trigonometry/analytical geometry.

Program:	**Young Authors Writing Camp**
Contact:	Mr. Joseph Miller, Director of Education and Youth Services
Address:	Young Authors Writing Camp Texas A&M University at Corpus Christi 6300 Ocean Dr., NRC 2200 Corpus Christi, TX 78412
Phone:	361-825-5777
Fax:	361-825-2778
Web site:	http://falcon.tamucc.edu/~outreach/acadprog.html
Program Type:	Academic Enrichment
Grade/Age Levels:	Grades 5–8
Description:	Students will learn to become independent, self-confident, and fluent authors through a variety of direct experiences. Students will use the university site as a way to generate ideas for their short stories, poems, letters, and other writing projects that they will create.

TEXAS

Program:	**Zoo Careers Camp**
Contact:	Ms. Laurie Craddock, Program Coordinator
Address:	Zoo Careers Camp 1989 Colonial Parkway Fort Worth, TX 76110
Phone:	817-759-7208
Fax:	817-759-7201
E-mail:	lcraddock@fortworthzoo.org
Web site:	http://www.fortworthzoo.org/school/summer_career.html
Program Type:	Academic Enrichment
Grade/Age Levels:	Rising grades 9–12
Description:	Campers investigate wildlife and zoo-related careers at the Fort Worth Zoo. The 5-day residential camp is a unique opportunity for high school students to experience many occupations in a world-class zoo. Campers learn about animal care, maintenance, training, and habitat conservation; accompany animal staff on daily schedules; participate in animal care activities; and attend presentations by zoo staff. This camp is designed to increase knowledge and skills about wildlife conservation, environmental and economic issues, initiatives, challenges, and success stories.

Program:	University of Utah Summer Mathematics Program for High School Students
Contact:	Ms. Angie Gardiner, Director of Undergraduate Services
Address:	University of Utah Department of Mathematics 155 South 1400 East, JWB 233 Salt Lake City, UT 84112-0090
Phone:	801-581-6851; 801-585-9478
Fax:	801-581-4148
E-mail:	gardiner@math.utah.edu
Web site:	http://www.math.utah.edu/hsp
Program Type:	Math, Sciences, Engineering, and Computer Science/Technology
Grade/Age Levels:	Grade 12
Description:	The Summer Mathematics Program for High School Students at the University of Utah provides outstanding students an opportunity to develop their talents to the fullest. By presenting intriguing puzzles, challenging problems, and powerful ideas, the program stimulates curiosity, develops the intellect, and lays a strong foundation for future work in mathematics, the sciences, or science related careers. In completing this 3-week program participants will receive three university credits in mathematics. All program costs are paid by a National Science Foundation VIGRE grant and the university's department of mathematics. Students who live far from the university may arrange to stay in the residence halls (there will be an additional cost). The prerequisite for the program is precalculus. Calculus is not required. Preference will be given to students between their junior and senior years.

UTAH

Program:	**University of Utah High School University Program**
Address:	University of Utah Office of Student Recruitment and High School Services 200 South Central Campus Dr., RM 80 Salt Lake City, UT 84112
Phone:	800-685-8856
Fax:	801-585-3257
Web site:	http://web.utah.edu/newstudents/hsup.htm
Program Type:	Academic Enrichment
Grade/Age Levels:	Grades 10–12
Description:	Students in this program earn university credits while enrolled in high school. Students are eligible to take any courses offered by the university. The program is offered in the fall, spring, and semester of each year. The University of Utah also offers an array of programs during the summer in its Continuing Education program. For a complete listing, visit http://www.smartkids.utha.edu.

Program:	**Future Leader Camp**
Address:	Future Leader Camp Norwich University 27 I.D. White Ave. Northfield, VT 05663
Phone:	802-485-2531; 800-468-6679
Fax:	802-485-2739
E-mail:	flc@norwick.edu
Web site:	http://www.norwich.edu/admissions/futureleader.html
Program Type:	Leadership/Service/Volunteer
Grade/Age Levels:	Rising grades 10 and up
Description:	The Future Leader Camp (FLC) is a 2-week summer program dedicated to developing the leadership potential of current high school students. FLC provides participants with a challenging and meaningful adventure camp experience while building an understanding of small group leadership techniques, leadership ethics, teamwork, problem solving and effective communication.

Program:	**UVM/GIV Engineering Summer Institute**
Contact:	Ms. Dawn Densmore, Director
Address:	UVM/GIV Engineering Summer Institute University of Vermont 33 Colchester Ave., Votey 101 Burlington, VT 05405
Phone:	802-656-8748
Fax:	802-656-8802
E-mail:	giv@sover.net; densmore@cems.uvm.edu
Web site:	http://www.cem.uvm.edu/summer/index.php
Program Type:	Math, Sciences, Engineering, and Computer Science/Technology; Academic Enrichment
Grade/Age Levels:	Rising grades 9 and up
Description:	Challenge yourself to think outside the box with a hands-on project, laboratory experiences, faculty presentations, and enlightening tours. You'll learn how technology impacts the human experience. Experience the thrill of creating sand arches at the beach and become part of an innovative team to work on one of the following diversified projects that will stretch your brain: Bio Mass Conversion, Wind Energy Conversion Systems, Robotics Technology, or Aeronautical Engineering. Students will be housed in campus dorms and will explore career opportunities and develop firsthand awareness of the nature of college life.

Program:	**Hollinsummer**
Address:	Hollinsummer Hollins University P.O. Box 9707 Roanoke, VA 24020-1707
Phone:	540-362-6401; 800-456-9595
Fax:	540-362-6218
E-mail:	huadm@hollins.edu
Web site:	http://www.hollins.edu
Program Type:	Academic Enrichment
Grade/Age Levels:	Grades 10–12
Description:	Hollinsummer is open to girls who are currently in grades 9–11. Students live on campus, take courses, and learn about the college search process. Girls choose 2 of 13 course offerings such as creative writing, leadership, modern dance, forensic chemistry, photography, and psychology. Cost includes 2-week residential stay (room and board), and other activities.

VIRGINIA

Program:	**Junior Engineering Technical Society (JETS)**
Contact:	Ms. Margaret Heaphy, Program Coordinator
Address:	Junior Engineering Technical Society 420 King St., Ste. 405 Alexandria, VA 22314
Phone:	703-548-5387 ext. 101
Fax:	703-548-0769
E-mail:	info@jets.org
Web site:	http://www.jets.org
Program Type:	Math, Sciences, Engineering, and Computer Science/Technology
Grade/Age Levels:	Grades 9–12
Description:	The Junior Engineering Technical Society (JETS) is a national nonprofit education organization that has served the precollege engineering community for more than 50 years. Through competitions and programs, JETS serves more than 40,000 students and 20,000 teachers, and holds programs on 150 college campuses each year. JETS promotes interest in engineering, science, mathematics, and technology, and is dedicated to providing real-world engineering and problem-solving experience to high school students. JETS programs challenge students to discover engineering in high school. JETS puts students in touch with engineers, shows them what engineers do, and demonstrates how the math and science concepts they are learning in class are applied in real life to engineering problems. JETS programs and resources get students involved with engineering and preparing for the future.

Program:	**Northern Virginia Writing Project Summer Institute**
Contact:	Mr. Mark Farrington
Address:	Northern Virginia Writing Project George Mason University Summer Institute NVWP/3E4 Fairfax, VA 22030-4444
Phone:	703-993-1168
E-mail:	mfarring@gmu.edu
Web site:	http://www.nvwp.org
Program Type:	Academic Enrichment
Grade/Age Levels:	Grades 5–12
Description:	The Northern Virginia Writing Project Summer Institute is an annual, 2-week writing enrichment program for approximately 100 selected students from grades 5–12 who come to the George Mason University campus to work with writing teachers and consultants. The writing produced in the Institute is published in an anthology and celebrated as a culminating event at the Institute.

VIRGINIA

Program:	Pre-Collegiate Summer Program in Early American History
Contact:	Dr. Carolyn Whittenburg, Director
Address:	Pre-Collegiate Summer Program in Early American History College of William and Mary National Institute of American History and Democracy P.O. Box 8795 Williamsburg, VA 23187-8795
Phone:	757-221-7652
E-mail:	precol@wm.edu
Web site:	http://www.wm.edu/niahd/precollegiate.php
Program Type:	Academic Enrichment
Grade/Age Levels:	Rising grades 11 and up
Description:	The National Institute of American History and Democracy (NIAHD) is a partnership between the College of William and Mary and the Colonial Williamsburg Foundation. It is dedicated to the study of the American past, material culture, and museums. The Institute sponsors The Pre-Collegiate Summer Program in Early American History, which includes 4 hours of academic credit. The program allows for students to experience a high degree of interaction with researchers in early American history.

Program:	**Presidential Classroom**
Contact:	Dr. Elizabeth Sherman, Executive Director
Address:	Presidential Classroom University of Virginia Georgetown University 119 Oronoco St. Alexandria, VA 22314
Phone:	703-683-5400; 202-464-5581
Fax:	703-548-5728
E-mail:	info@presidentialclassroom.org
Web site:	http://www.presidentialclassroom.org
Program Type:	Leadership/Service/Volunteer
Grade/Age Levels:	Grades 9–12
Description:	Presidential Classroom, a premiere nonprofit, nonpartisan, youth leadership organization hosts top high school students from around the world on Georgetown University campus for one "action-packed" week. There are many sessions to choose from—Communications and Journalism, Law and Justice, PC Scholars, Science and Technology, Global Business, National Security, and Future World Leaders Summit—all designed to pique students' interests.

VIRGINIA

Program:	**Research Science Institute (RSI)**
Contact:	Maite Ballestero, Vice President, Programs
Address:	Research Science Institute Massachusetts Institute of Technology Center for Excellence in Education 8201 Greensboro Dr., Ste. 215 McLean, VA 22102
Phone:	703-448-9662
Fax:	703-448-9068
E-mail:	cee@cee.org; rsi@cee.org
Web site:	http://www.cee.org/rsi/index.shtml
Program Type:	Math, Sciences, Engineering, and Computer Science/Technology; Academic Enrichment; Internships/Paid Positions
Grade/Age Levels:	Grade 11
Description:	Research Science Institute (RSI) is an intense summer program in which some of the most talented high school students from the U.S. and around the world come together to do cutting-edge science and mathematics research. Living on the MIT campus, they do research projects under the guidance of mentors from the university and area institutions and corporations. RSI is open to students who have completed the third year of high school, or the equivalent. Program application deadline is early February.

Program:	**Science Training and Research Program (S.T.A.R.)**
Contact:	Dr. Vernon Hurte, Program Director
Address:	Science Training and Research Program College of William and Mary Office of Multicultural Affairs P.O. Box 8795 Campus Center, Room 107 Williamsburg, VA 23187-8795
Phone:	757-221-2300
Fax:	757-221-1105
E-mail:	vjhurt@wm.edu
Web site:	http://www.wm.edu/multiculturalaffairs/starprogram.php
Program Type:	Math, Sciences, Engineering, and Computer Science/Technology
Grade/Age Levels:	Rising grade 11
Description:	The Science Training and Research Program (S.T.A.R.) is a precollegiate summer enrichment program for rising 11th grade students from disadvantaged backgrounds. Because such students are often unaware of the rich and varied opportunities available to them in the sciences, this unique program is designed to introduce students to the world of science, research, and technology. Twenty-five students will be selected to participate in this 4-week residential program at the College of William and Mary.

VIRGINIA

Program:	**Shenandoah Conservatory Performing Arts Camp**
Address:	Shenandoah Conservatory Performing Arts Camp Shenandoah University 1460 University Dr. Winchester VA 22601-5195
Phone:	540-545-7210
Fax:	540-665-5402
Web site:	http://www.su.edu/ShenandoahPerforms/Camp
Program Type:	Fine, Performing, and Visual Arts
Grade/Age Levels:	Ages 12–18
Description:	The Performing Arts Camp of Shenandoah Conservatory provides middle and high school students the opportunity to hone their artistic skills through participation in a variety of small and large ensembles, and instruction from world-class faculty. We have programs in band, orchestra, choir, jazz, dance, harp, and piano. Students also participate in eurhythmics class and a technology class. This is both a residential and commuter program.

Program:	University of Virginia (UVA) Saturday and Summer Enrichment Program
Contact:	Dr. Stephanie Ferguson, Director
Address:	Saturday and Summer Enrichment Program University of Virginia P.O. Box 400264 405 Emmet St. S. Charlottesville, VA 22904-4264
Phone:	434-924-3182
Fax:	434-924-1483
E-mail:	curry-sep@virginia.edu
Web site:	http://curry.edschool.virginia.edu/go/enrich
Program Type:	Academic Enrichment
Grade/Age Levels:	Grades 5–11
Description:	UVA's Summer Enrichment Program provides extended study in liberal arts, fine arts, social sciences, math, science, and technology. Cost includes tuition, room and board, and materials. Need based scholarships are available.

VIRGINIA

Program:	University of Virginia Summer Language Institute
Address:	Summer Language Institute University of Virginia P.O. Box 400161 Charlottesville, VA 22904-4161
Phone:	434-924-3371
Fax:	434-924-1483
E-mail:	uvasli@virginia.edu
Web site:	http://www.virginia.edu/summer/SLI
Program Type:	Academic Enrichment
Grade/Age Levels:	Rising grades 11–12
Description:	The University of Virginia's Summer Language Institute offers 9-week programs in French, German, Italian, Latin, Russian, Spanish, Tibetan and Chinese in a near-immersion environment. These eight programs are designed to serve people who wish to attain an intermediate level of competence in a new language in just one summer. Students who successfully complete the program earn 12 credits, the equivalent of 2 academic years of language study at the college level. Participants attend classes 5 days a week, for 7.5 hours a day. The limited class size allows for individualized and group instruction not usually available in standard language classrooms.

Program:	**University of Virginia Young Writers Workshop**
Contact:	Ms. Margo Figgins, Director
Address:	Young Writers Workshop The University of Virginia The Curry School P.O. Box 400273 Charlottesville, VA 22903
Phone:	434-924-0836
Fax:	434-924-0747
E-mail:	writers@virginia.edu
Web site:	http://fusion.web.virginia.edu/yww/index.cfm
Program Type:	Academic Enrichment; Fine, Performing, and Visual Arts
Grade/Age Levels:	Rising grades 9–12
Description:	The Young Writers Workshop of the University of Virginia, established in 1982, brings together a community of writers with a common purpose: to create a supportive and noncompetitive environment where teenagers can live and work as artists. Every staff member has a commitment to writing. The faculty, professional authors interested in developing new talent, bring practical experience to the workshop setting.

VIRGINIA

Program:	**Virginia Association of Soil and Water Conservation Youth Conservation Camp**
Contact:	Ms. Dana Roberts, Camp Director
Address:	Virginia Association of Soil and Water Conservation Youth Conservation Camp Virginia Tech 7308 Hanover Green Dr., Ste. 100 Mechanicsville, VA 23111
Phone:	804-559-0324
Fax:	804-559-0325
E-mail:	dana.roberts@vaswcd.org
Web site:	http://www.vaswcd.org/youthcamp.htm
Program Type:	Math, Sciences, Engineering, and Computer Science/Technology
Grade/Age Levels:	Grades 9–12
Description:	For 30 years, the Virginia Association of Soil and Water Conservation Districts has sponsored a weeklong summer conservation camp for Virginia high school students on the campus of Virginia Tech. The program brings together about 90 interested students for a week of learning about Virginia's natural resources from conservation professionals and faculty from Virginia Tech. Most of the instruction is hands-on and outdoors.

Program:	**Virginia Tech Summer Music Camp**
Contact:	Mr. David Widder, Director
Address:	Summer Music Camp Virginia Tech Music Department Blacksburg, VA 24061-0240
Phone:	540-231-5685
Fax:	540-231-5034
E-mail:	David.Widder@vt.edu
Web site:	http://www.music.vt.edu/outreach/camp
Program Type:	Fine, Performing, and Visual Arts
Grade/Age Levels:	Grades 7–10
Description:	Sponsored by the music department, these band, jazz band, and chamber ensembles for students focus on the development of individual musical skills together with regular and extensive contact with professional educators and musicians. Classes in conducting, jazz, improvisation, composition, and computer applications in music, along with private lessons also are available. Program includes both a residential and commuter option.

VIRGINIA

VIRGINIA

Program:	**Virginia Tech Summer Training Academy for Rising Students (VT STARS)**
Contact:	Mr. Edward McPherson, Director
Address:	The Virginia Tech Summer Training Academy for Rising Students Virginia Polytechnic Institute and State University Torgersen Hall 3025—Mail Code 0232 Blacksburg, VA 24061
Phone:	540-231-2436
Fax:	540-231-5922
E-mail:	vtstars@vt.edu
Web site:	http://www.vtstars.vt.edu
Program Type:	Math, Sciences, Engineering, and Computer Science/Technology, Academic Enrichment
Grade/Age Levels:	Grades 9–12
Description:	VT STARS strives to be a regional model for rural and urban high schools to motivate and increase the number of female, minority, and underrepresented students seeking enrollment in post secondary degree programs and jobs in scientific, technical-related career paths. This summer residency program has a selective enrollment. Closed enrollment is for students in the "academic middle" who have yet to realize their potential for academic excellence.

Program:	Cybercamps
Address:	Giant Campus, Inc./Cybercamps, 3101 Western Ave., Ste. 100, Seattle, WA 98121
Phone:	206-442-4500; 888-904-2267
Fax:	206-442-4501
E-mail:	info@giantcampus.com
Web site:	http://www.cybercamps.com
Program Type:	Math, Sciences, Engineering, and Computer Science/Technology
Grade/Age Levels:	Ages 7–18
Description:	Cybercamps offer camps at 50 locations nationwide to teach students technology-related skills. Both single and multiweek, residential and commuter programs are available. Courses have included game design, animation, video production, robotics, and Web design. The well-rounded courses introduce specific projects and activities showing young people many different types of technology and how they work. Visit our Web site to find your nearest location.

WASHINGTON

Program:	**Salish Summer Sailing and Science Expeditions**
Contact:	Ms. Lori Mitchell, Education Director
Address:	Salish Summer Sailing and Science Expeditions, Salish Sea Expeditions, 647 Horizon View Pl. NW, Bainbridge Island, WA 98110
Phone:	206-780-7848
Fax:	206-780-9007
E-mail:	info@salish.org
Web site:	http://www.salish.org
Program Type:	Math, Sciences, Engineering, and Computer Science/Technology
Grade/Age Levels:	Grades 6–12
Description:	Salish Sea Expeditions was founded in 1996 to inspire a passion for exploring, understanding, and respecting the marine environment through hands-on scientific inquiry. Since then, more than 4,000 middle and high school students and 1,000 teachers have sailed the waters of Puget Sound as students of our innovative "science-under-sail" programs aboard the 61-foot sailing research vessel.

Program:	**Summer Institute for Mathematics at the University of Washington (SIMUW)**
Address:	Summer Institute for Mathematics at the University of Washington Department of Mathematics University of Washington Box 354350 Seattle, WA 98195-4350
Phone:	206-399-1014
Fax:	206-543-0397
E-mail:	simuw@math.washington.edu
Web site:	http://www.math.washington.edu/~simuw/2007/index.html
Program Type:	Math, Sciences, Engineering, Computer Science, and Technology
Grade/Age Levels:	Rising grade 12
Description:	Open to residents of Washington, British Columbia, Oregon, Idaho, or Alaska who have completed 3 years of high school mathematics including algebra, geometry, and trigonometry.

Getting a glimpse of the depth and beauty of mathematics can be a transforming experience for a student, whatever interests the student may intend to pursue in the future. The Summer Institute for Mathematics at the University of Washington is intended to provide talented, enthusiastic students with just such a glimpse. The mathematical topics studied are accessible, yet of sufficient sophistication to be challenging, allowing students to participate in the experience of mathematical inquiry and be immersed in the world of mathematics.

Other UW resources and programs for elementary, middle, and high school students are located at http://www.outreach.washington.edu/syp/otherUW.asp#high.

WASHINGTON

Program:	**Mountain State University Forensics Science Camp**
Contact:	Mr. Roger Teets, Director of Forensic Investigation
Address:	Mountain University Box 9003 Beckley, WV 25802
Phone:	304-929-1467
E-mail:	rteets@mountainstate.edu
Web site:	http://www.mountainstate.edu/majors/whystudy/forensics/PDF/summercamp2006.pdf
Program Type:	Math, Sciences, Engineering, and Computer Science/Technology
Grade/Age Levels:	Grades 11–12
Description:	A learning experience for high school students who are interested in pursuing a degree in forensic investigation. This program offers students an introduction in locating, identifying, collecting, preserving, and interpreting physical evidence at crime scenes. It includes classroom instruction and interaction and hands-on skills.

Program:	West Virginia Wesleyan Summer Gifted Camp
Contact:	Dr. Joseph Wiest, Director
Address:	West Virginia Wesleyan College Box 89 Buckhannon, WV 26201
Phone:	304-473-8072
Fax:	304-472-2571
E-mail:	sgp@wvwc.edu
Web site:	http://www.wvwc.edu/wvwc/gifted/giftcamp.html
Program Type:	Academic Enrichment
Grade/Age Levels:	Grades 5–11
Description:	The Wesleyan Summer Gifted Program has the objective of placing bright young students with academic scholars to enable students to study academic subjects at a deeper level, and acquire an appreciation of the liberal arts.

- Beginning program for fifth and sixth-grade students focuses on physics, biology, nature, math, and literature of Jules Verne.
- Beginning program for seventh and eighth-grade students focuses on interrelationships among math, science, and computer skills.
- Intermediate program for seventh and eighth-grade students focuses on geometry, physics, and basic computer programming language, in addition to creative writing and a study of China.
- Advanced program for 9th and 10th graders focuses on calculus, analog and digital electronics, and advanced computer programming languages and applications, in addition to creative writing and a study of China.
- The College Prep Program for 10th and 11th graders completion will result in 2 semester hours of college credit. The focus will be on science of astrophysics, an introduction to calculus, and creative writing and literature.

WEST VIRGINIA

Program:	**Archaeology Public Field School**
Contact:	Jean Dowiasch, Education Coordinator
Address:	Archaeology Public Field School University of Wisconsin-La Crosse Mississippi Valley Archeology Center 1725 State St. La Crosse, WI 54601
Phone:	608-785-8454
Fax:	608-785-6474
E-mail:	dowiasch.jean@uwlax.edu
Web site:	http://www.uwlax.edu/mvac
Program Type:	Academic Enrichment
Grade/Age Levels:	Grades 9–12
Description:	Students participate in an actual archaeological excavation by working alongside professional archaeologists in the field. Campers take part in small-scale excavations (test units) and survey work. Lab work may include washing ceramics, stone tools, and other remains, and sorting them into basic categories. No previous experience is necessary.

Program:	Lake Superior Pathfinders Program
Contact:	Elizabeth Post, Program Director
Address:	Lake Superior Pathfinders Program Northland College Environmental Career Programs 1411 Ellis Ave. Ashland, WI 54806-3999
Phone:	715-682-1699
Web site:	http://www.northland.edu/Northland/soei/ Programs/Pathfinders.htm
Program Type:	Leadership/Service/Volunteer
Grade/Age Levels:	Grades 8–12
Description:	Be one of the selected high school students who will live and learn on Lake Superior, the world's largest freshwater lake! Learn more about your personal leadership style using low and high ropes courses and climbing walls that offer safe, but challenging activities to build your skills. Be immersed in the Lake Superior environment; explore its estuaries; kayak to its sea caves; investigate Lake Superior's critical issues based on a sustainable model that balances social, environmental, and economic perspectives; and interact with Chippewa tribal elders and educators as they share their culture. Join your peers to learn with guest speakers, community leaders, and Northland College's Sigurd Olson Environmental Institute and University of Wisconsin-Extension educators, faculty, and field counselors; develop knowledge to help you take action on environmental issues; and lodge at Northland College's Environmental Living and Learning Center dormitory, located in Ashland, WI (some nights are spent camping on secluded Lake Superior beaches).

WISCONSIN

Program:	**Milwaukee School of Engineering Summer Programs**
Contact:	Ms. Linda Levandowski
Address:	MSOE Summer Programs Milwaukee School of Engineering 1025 N. Broadway Milwaukee, WI 53202-3109
Phone:	800-332-6763
E-mail:	explore@msoe.edu
Web site:	http://www.msoe.edu/admiss/summer.html
Program Type:	Academic Enrichment
Grade/Age Levels:	Grades 9–12
Description:	This weeklong summer camp will challenge you to learn more about a specific career field: architectural engineering/building construction; biomedical engineering; computer engineering/software engineering; electrical engineering; mechanical engineering/industrial engineering/nursing; business; or technical communication. You will get hands-on exposure by working in our labs on exciting projects. Working closely with MSOE faculty and current students is an integral part of the program. MSOE offers five programs that quickly fill up: Discover the Possibilities, Focus on the Possibilities, Focus on Business, Focus on Nursing, and Focus on Technical Communication.

Program:	University of Wisconsin-Milwaukee Architecture Summer Camp
Contact:	Ms. Tammy Taylor, Camp Assistant Director
Address:	Architecture Summer Camp University of Wisconsin-Milwaukee School of Architecture and Urban Planning P.O. Box 413 Milwaukee, WI 53201-0413
Phone:	414-229-5821; 414-229-4015
Fax:	414-229-6976
E-mail:	ttaylor@uwm.edu
Web site:	http://www.uwm.edu/SARUP/architecture/ summercamp/index.html
Program Type:	Academic Enrichment
Grade/Age Levels:	Grades 9–12
Description:	This precollege program is designed to introduce high school students to careers in architecture. Students participate in morning studios, similar to those in college architecture courses, and attend various supplemental activities such as trips to architecture firms and walking tours of the city. The weeklong program is limited to 30 students.

WISCONSIN

Program:	**Wisconsin Center for Academically Talented Youth (WCATY) Summer Programs**
Contact:	Mr. Scott Lein or Ms. Rebecca Vonesh, Program Director
Address:	Wisconsin Center for Academically Talented Youth 2909 Landmark Pl. Madison, WI 53713
Phone:	608-271-1617
Fax:	608-271-8080
E-mail:	info@wcaty.org
Web site:	http://www.wcaty.org
Program Type:	Academic Enrichment; Math, Sciences, Engineering, and Computer Science/Technology; Fine, Performing, and Visual Arts
Grade/Age Levels:	Grades 3–12
Description:	WCATY offers several programs for talented children and youth, including:

- *Summer Transitional Enrichment Program* (STEP) for grades 7–8;
- *Young Students Summer Program* (YSSP) for grades 3–6;
- *Accelerated Learning Program* (ALP) for grades 9–12;
- *Career & College Planning & Exploration Program* (CCPEP);
- The *Young Scholar Project Program* is a competitive grant program for seventh and eighth grade Midwest Academic Talent Search participants.
- *District Co-op Courses* feature online discussions and face-to-face workshops that allow students across a region or school district to learn together.

Program:	**Teton Science Schools**
Address:	Teton Science Schools 700 Coyote Canyon Rd. Jackson, WY 83001
Phone:	307-733-1313
Fax:	307-733-7560
E-mail:	info@tetonscience.org
Web site:	http://www.tetonscience.org
Program Type:	Math, Sciences, Engineering, and Computer Science/Technology
Grade/Age Levels:	Grades 6–12
Description:	Join students from around the country on an educational adventure exploring field research, natural history, and backcountry experiences in the Greater Yellowstone/Geo-ecosystem. The camp provides in-residence programming for high school and middle school students. High School Field Ecology has been Teton Science Schools' flagship summer program for students interested in ecology and applied field research. Additional programs include Field Natural History, Middle School Field Ecology, and Young Women in Natural Resource Management.

Program:	**University of Wyoming Engineering Summer Program**
Address:	Engineering Summer Program University of Wyoming College of Engineering Dept. 3295 1000 E. University Ave. Laramie, WY 82071
Phone:	307-766-4253
E-mail:	enginfo@uwyo.edu
Web site:	http://wwweng.uwyo.edu/highschool/esp
Program Type:	Math, Sciences, Engineering, and Computer Science/Technology
Grade/Age Levels:	Grade 11
Description:	The College of Engineering and the Wyoming Engineering Society, in conjunction with the J. Kenneth & Pat Kennedy Endowment, offer high school juniors an opportunity to participate in a summer program of hands-on experiences in various engineering fields. Students participate in laboratory sessions, working one-on-one with faculty members and graduate students on projects such as building digital circuits or developing solutions to environmental problems.

Program:	University of Wyoming Summer High School Institute
Contact:	Mr. Duncan Harris, Director
Address:	Summer High School Institute University of Wyoming Dept. 4147, 101 Merica 1000 E. University Ave. Laramie, WY 82071
Phone:	307-766-3005
Fax:	307-766-4298
E-mail:	hsi@uwyo.edu
Web site:	http://uwadmnweb.uwyo.edu/Provost/hsi
Program Type:	Academic Enrichment
Grade/Age Levels:	Grade 10
Description:	The mission of the Summer High School Institute is to provide a place where some of the state's most intellectually talented sophomores can gather before their junior and senior years, living and studying in an environment with no pressure for grades, and sharing ideas and friendship with other gifted students. Students at this 3-week residential camp study courses such as weather and aviation, folk tales, exercise physiology, stage combat, hip-hop and society, robotic engineering, and many other courses.

INDEX OF OPPORTUNITIES BY PROGRAM TYPE

Fine, Performing, and Visual Arts

Gap Year/Study Abroad/ International Travel

Internships/Paid Positions

Math, Sciences, Engineering, and Computer Science/Technology

Leadership/Service/Volunteer

ABOUT THE AUTHOR

Sandra L. Berger has been a citizen activist and advocate for gifted children for more than 30 years. She originally was led down this path by her own gifted youngsters. Berger holds a master's degree in gifted education curriculum and instruction with training in counseling. For 15 years, she was the gifted education information specialist at the ERIC Clearinghouse on Disabilities and Gifted Education and the AskERIC system, responding to thousands of questions about gifted and special education. She is a member of the editorial advisory board and a technology columnist for *Understanding Our Gifted*, has authored numerous articles in the field of gifted education, and shares her views on college planning and gifted education through participation in national, regional, and state conferences. Berger and her husband of 46 years currently have 4 grandchildren.